CHRISTIANITY CLOSE TO LIFE

Rita F. Snowden – apart from her books – is widely known in many countries. After six years at business, she trained as a deaconess of the New Zealand Methodist Church, serving in turn two pioneer country areas before moving to the largest city for several years of social work during an economic depression. Whilst bedridden with a severe heart condition, she wrote her first book, *Through Open Windows*.

Her extensive travels include five years touring New Zealand, lecturing and introducing books. In Australia she was the guest speaker at the Methodist Centenary in Queensland and, some years later, at the Methodist Home Mission Centenary in New South Wales; in a similar working capacity she visited other Australian states including the primitive Inland. She has also travelled widely in Europe, Palestine, the Middle East and Japan.

Miss Snowden has served the world Church – beyond the ministry of her own denomination – with regular broadcasting commitments. She has written and spoken in Britain, Canada and the United States, and in Tonga at the invitation of Queen Salote. She has represented her Church at the World Methodist Conference in Oxford, later being elected the first woman Vice-president of the New Zealand Methodist Church, and President of its Deaconess Association. She is an Hon. Vice-president of the New Zealand Women Writers' Society, a Fellow of the International Institute of Arts and Letters and a member of P.E.N. A long-time contributor to *The British Weekly, The Methodist Recorder* and other periodicals in the English-speaking world, she is the author of more than fifty books for adults and children, her most recent being *When Sorrow Comes*, and the companion volumes: *A Woman's Book of Prayers, Prayers for the Family, Where the Action Is, Prayers in Later Life, More Prayers for* ̶̶̶̶̶̶ ̶̶̶̶̶̶ ̶̶̶̶̶̶ *̶e̶.*

Miss S̶ ̶̶̶̶̶̶ ̶̶̶̶̶̶ O.B.E.

D1612978

RITA F. SNOWDEN

CHRISTIANITY CLOSE TO LIFE

COLLINS
Fount Paperbacks

First published in Fount Paperbacks 1978

© Rita F. Snowden 1978

Made and printed in Great Britain by
William Collins Sons & Co Ltd, Glasgow

To my friend
R. H. Grenville

'Ordinary people, if they want religion at all,
want it to live by, and not merely to think about.'

Dr. W. R. Maltby

CONTENTS

INTRODUCTION

I learned early to test a thing by the touchstone : 'Is it practical?' So when first I consciously approached religion, this was a question that asked for an answer.

Soon, I discovered love, wonder, joy and beauty were tied to practicality. I began with the first page of the Bible, where God is proclaimed practical. 'God said, "Let there be light"; and there was light. And God saw that the light was good.' (Genesis 1, verses 3-4).

And to this hour it remains a wonder – as my friend, R. H. Grenville, to whom this book is dedicated, reminds me :

> Nothing is more beautiful than light,
> the first-created.
> Something in the very core of earth
> remembers the long night through which it waited,
> shadowed and shapeless, colourless, until
> the Word was spoken :
> 'Let there be light !' and light streamed forth and
> sang for exaltation.

It is not unfitting that one's knowledge of God should be practical; or that it should be present-day. Monica Furlong, English journalist – breathing much the same air we do – said in the *Daily Mail* on 24 December 1962 : 'I had an experience of God so vivid and so shattering that I knew that either God existed, or I must be stark, staring mad. And I didn't feel mad, only much happier than I had ever felt in my life before . . . The brief moment I refer to seemed, and still seems to me, the most real thing in my life.'

I can say as much of my own experience. My family regularly occupied a pew in the little Wesleyan Chapel, a hop-and-a-skip distant from home. I was seldom absent, but nobody guessed the questions in my mind – I was suffering from 'spiritual growing-pains'. Augustine had expressed my state in straightforward words, as a member of God's world-family: 'O Lord, Thou hast made me for Thyself; and my heart is restless until I find my rest in Thee'. I was more than body, like the wild creatures about me; or body and mind; *I was body, mind and spirit.*

An evangelist came – and people from the church, and chapel, and some lacking allegiance of any kind, gathered in the village hall, to listen to what he had to tell us of the Kingdom of God. But I was determined not to be 'stormed into it'. I persuaded myself to wait for a time that I believed would come when my questing mind, and my emotions, would be in accord.

And it came. Alone in my little room, I offered to God my whole youthful personality; and, as suddenly and as really as relief and joy came to one who once travelled the Damascus Road, it came to me. I felt there and then a shine upon my very face. I knew myself too shy to speak of it to any in my family – but it was a miracle, and it changed my life. I had dealings with God – I lived in His wonderful world – I answered to His ever-expanding purposes!

Surely, this is practical enough to set the start of our enquiry. We can safely by-pass the claim of the agnostic, that, 'It is *impossible* to know God, because of His infinite nature, His absoluteness, His spirituality'. If we know only these few things, added to what is revealed of Him on the first page of Genesis, we already know much, so He can't be altogether unknowable. Only a schoolboy – who hasn't yet had time to devote to these matters – can be excused for asking, as one did lately in a book with a Foreword by the Archbishop of Canterbury, Dr Coggan:

> Who is God?
>   What is God?
> Is He really true?
>   Does He work wonders?
> I wish I knew.

Is He in the green trees?
Is He in the meadow?
Is He in the latest beat?
Is He in the twisting feet?
Is He real?
Oh! I say! I wish I knew.

No one of us can claim to know God fully — that we cannot even claim of a long-time friend. But we have much to share!

Religion is not just a matter of feeling; or of being in a familiar pew at eleven or seven on a Sunday. It covers the whole of life. It is not something that makes a little difference to a few things: but something which makes all the difference to everything. As practical as that!

1. BUT DO I REALLY WANT TO FIND GOD?

Sitting quietly writing my book in English (because I can do no other) I am fascinated to find – when I lift over my giant *Britannica World Language Dictionary* from the shelf nearest my elbow – that the equivalent of the word 'practical' is firmly established in each of the six other languages there. So important it is! In French, it is *pratique*; in German, *praktisch*; in Italian, *practico*; in Spanish, *práctico*; in Swedish, *praktisk*; in Yiddish, *praktish.*

In the business of getting to know another, it seems, one can proceed from a number of points. *First, there are actions of this unknown that I can watch; and results of his past work that I can examine.* And gradually I have come to realize that it is the same with God. I can watch His actions in the world around me, daily; and in nature, history and human relationship, examine His past work through the centuries. Neither is remote to my purpose. Good St Francis de Sales early discovered that – and was not the first one to do so. Said he, setting it down beautifully, 'Just as the birds, wherever they fly, always encounter the air, so wherever we go or wherever we are, we find God present. Everyone knows this truth, but everyone,' he felt obliged to add, 'is not attentive to grasp it.' Many of us go upon our way without really knowing God, His creation, and daily providence, despite extra knowledge from modern books, radio, films, TV, reproducing colour photographs from under the sea; and from men travelling in outer space, and walking on the moon. God's universe is not only ancient, but immense.

The second source of information concerning another can be sayings of his, preserved, and sayings of others concerning him. Autobiographies, diaries, journals and biographies count here. And it is the same, it seems, with God; so I turn with a new readiness to the Scriptures of the Old and New Testaments, where are recorded sayings of His, and recorded sayings of men and women about Him, collected through the ages. They differ, of course, as greatly as, say, the works of Chaucer at the birthtime of our language and the modern command and grace of Churchill; the writing of Agatha Christie and the poetry of T. S. Eliot or John Betjeman. In Scripture even more literary forms are employed – old-world story, history, drama, parable, poetry, biography, song, sermon, letters. And amidst this glorious variety are matters baldly secular – like court-reports and government issues – and others as sacred as prayers, and as secret as aspirations, and sins unconfessed. So, all kinds of allowances have to be made in approaching the reading of Scripture. But there, one discovers, awaits an amazing vitality. To instance but one, born in my own birth-year, John Lawrence made that discovery. And there is nothing like it! Educated first at Eton, then at Oxford, he qualified later as a lawyer, later still reading French, Russian and Italian fluently, and German and Spanish less so. He married; and in that critical war-year, 1939, that changed life for so many of us, worked with the German-Jewish Aid Committee. In time, he joined the BBC; then he became the first British Press Attaché in the USSR. Such appointments represented a lot of living; but I need not add to my thumb-nail sketch – Sir John Lawrence became widely known as a thoroughly-awake modern leader. 'When', said he tellingly, 'the last glow of Faith faded from the horizon, the world seemed by contrast, inexpressibly cold and dreary . . . Then I considered the fact that if nothing was proved, equally nothing was disproved . . . So I got out my Greek Testament, and began to read . . . *After that, I was over the top of the hill.*' To this practical discovery of his, one might add the witness of many another.

A third realization is that no one approach is more likely than another to enable one to know another person. Or, for that matter, to know God. There is no line drawn between things sacred, and secular, between what can come in company, or in isolation. On this point, I find James Martineau asking pointedly : 'Where then is your God? . . . You say, "He is everywhere." Then show me *anywhere* that you have seen Him . . . These are the testing questions by which', he concludes, 'we may learn whether *we too* – like the Agnostics in Athens – have raised our altar to an "Unknown God".'

Considering now these ways of getting to know another – and God – I find myself more often, and more gladly, repeating the words of schoolmaster L. P. Jacks: 'In Whom do I live, and move and have my being? *In Him.* Whose the vitality of the air I draw in with every breath? *His.* Whose the pressure of the atmosphere, fifteen pounds avoirdupois to every square inch of my body? *His.* Whose the firm support of the ground under my feet, and the light of consciousness wherewith I am conscious of it? *His.* In Whose light do I see what is visible, in Whose sound hear what is audible, in Whose strength do what is do-able? *In His.* Who keeps my heart beating from moment to moment and the blood coursing through my veins? *He Who keeps the earth spinning on its axis, the fires burning in the sun, and Orion on his steady march amid the constellations; He Who paves the Milky Way with millions of worlds.* Awful thoughts, my masters, and tremendous facts!'

To lay hold of such, is to come by a new respect for one's capacity as a person; to feel oneself held, not merely holding on to life; to know a new inward peace, and purpose. These add up to religion's practicality! I am trying to set down this miracle in prose – many have expressed it in poetry. I will restrain from quoting poets as freely as I might, because I know that for some, poetry does not speak as clearly as prose. Though curiously, much of the world's most compelling witness of God's awareness, up through the years, has come to us by way of the Psalms, *in poetry.*

To be sure, the framework of our lives and those of the psalmists is not the same. We live today in a different world – thousands of years later, with different thought-patterns. But underneath, in the things of the heart, where most of all we live, little is changed – friendship, love, self-forgetfulness hold; and pride, hate, and dim shades of doubt exist as ever. Where is anything more real than the words in which the psalmists *speak of God – and speak to God?*

They were not all saints, or minstrels on their way up to religious festivals. Far from it – they were ordinary folk, toilers most, knowing the passions we know. Some were of the country with its hills, trees and patchwork plains; some of the city with its crowds; some went down to the sea in ships, and did business in great waters. But wherever life met them, day in, day out, their words rose vibrant with reality. They were not like the heathen, blindly feeling out after God, if haply they might find Him. They uttered the cry of sorrow, raised the voice of indignation, or uncovered the soul's secret urge, or the glory of praise and exultation, and their words did not come back from the void – they awakened a loving response *in the heart of the Eternal.*

But to face more closely the awkward question : suppose you or I *do not want to find God? Or to be found of Him?* It may be that we fear He will too greatly interfere with our chosen way of life. Another point as real may be that we are not interested in the *kind* of God He is – if we can judge by other people's worship, and daily witness. 'The question at stake', to use Dr E. F. Scott's words, 'is that of our conception of Him. Are we to think of Him grudging us our earthly life, or are we to find in it a proof of His presence and goodness?'

Some of us find it pridefully satisfying to claim intellectual difficulties; though, in truth, few of us are really held back from awareness of God by the problems of our little minds. More likely, our self-centredness, or 'moral dug-outs' are the bother; or like our distinguished storyteller, Katherine Mansfield, amidst ill-health, and relationships complex, divided opinions do it. 'God is now gone for us all', said she. 'Yet we must carry our weakness, and our sin, and our devilishness to somebody.'

I was shy of God from the start – even afraid of Him. My thoughts, it was soon plain, were largely coloured by Old Testament pictures in the family Bible – and I didn't want to have anything to do with Him. Heavily-bearded and stern, He was pictured either handing down the pillars of stone which were the Ten Commandments, or dealing as firmly, on some other occasion, with His chosen people, at war or at worship. But a time came, of course, when I began to echo my youthful modern equivalent of Job's words : 'O that I knew where I might find Him!'

No less a beloved person in our day than Dr John Baillie – to whom so many of us owe so much – has come to us confessing his slowness in finding God. *'Because'*, said he, *'I did not want to find Him!* Part of the reason why I could not (or thought I could not) hear Him speak, was that He was saying some things to me which I did not wish to hear.'

Many of us, it seems, start off on the wrong foot, in our spiritual pilgrimage, because we do not accept the fact that He is all that Jesus declared Him to be.

C. S. Lewis – another of our day – university lecturer, and in time, popular story-teller and Christian writer, wanted nothing to do with God. In his widely-read and appreciated autobiography, *Surprised by Joy*, he says : 'You must picture me alone in that room in Magdalen, night after night, feeling, whenever my mind lifted even for a second from my work, the steady, unrelenting approach of *Him Whom I so earnestly desired not to meet* . . . In the Trinity Term of 1929 I gave in, and admitted that God was God, and knelt and prayed : perhaps, that night, the most dejected and reluctant convert in all England. I did not then see what is now the most shining and obvious thing; the Divine humility which will accept a convert even on such terms.'

Chay Blyth – welcomed back to Britain a little while ago by members of the Royal Family, the Prime Minister, and a great company of admirers, left no one in doubt about his position. At thirty-one, a former Army Sergeant of the Parachute Division, he had set out from Hamble, on the previous 18 October (1970). Since that time, he had made the *fastest* non-stop voyage round the world, in his single-handed ketch *British Steel*. More than that, he had sailed two-hundred-and-ninety-two days, *the only man ever to sail from East to West, against prevailing winds*.

With that understanding behind him, those present

might have expected him to respond to their welcome back with considerable pride. But no – those gathered there that day heard words reported to the rest of us later: 'When you get the rough seas coming at you, it doesn't take very long to put you in your place.' And in his diary, shared later, he wrote: *'No one will ever say to me there is no God.* To atheists, I say, "Go sailing single-handed for a few weeks, and *let me know then*".'

Where is a more practical approach?

2. WHERE CAN I START TO FIND GOD?

There is no one answer, I think, to that.

I was struck by three words I found when I visited Ambleside, in the beautiful English Lake District, with its sturdy hills, its streets, houses, shops, old stone churches graced with trees – its little crooked ways inviting.

Under a great tree, I found a framed map of the District, which said, aided by a pointer: YOU ARE HERE!

And in answer to this question: 'Where can I start to find God?', I am persuaded to offer each reader of this practical book the same answer: 'You are here! This is the starting place!'

Growing-up, loving God's created world of nature, hills, trees, streams and creatures, it wasn't surprising that I started to seek God *in Nature*. It was only years later – when as a young adult I held my first book of Theology in my hand, at a lecture – that I actually found as much suggested in print. (I was even surprised that it wasn't an original idea.) The book went on to suggest that I would make three discoveries: *that this world was created in Time*; that it was clearly *created by an intelligent mind*; that it was as certainly *created for a great purpose*.

Not all, I have found, start at that point, though Dr Leslie Weatherhead – priding himself on being modern – makes room in his book, *The Christian Agnostic*, to say: 'For myself, the old argument which seeks to prove God's existence from design, if rather differently stated, is still convincing.'

The old argument, about how long it took Him to create the world, no longer seems important – some literalists read the 'six days' to be six days as we know them; others of us, speaking the language taught us by modern science, are more likely to say, 'a multiple of six million years'. The more one knows of His many ways of working, the more one marvels – but all the time He is the intelligent, dependable Creator. When Darwin heard that in Madagascar there was an orchid with a spur eleven inches long, his immediate response was that somewhere there must be a moth with a proboscis of that length to pollinate the flowers. His study of creation had shown him that things of this sort were not accidental, or erratic. Some, listening in, laughed at him; but forty years on, a night-flying moth with a twelve-inch tongue, *Xanthopan morgani praedicta*, was discovered on the island.

Without a certain dependability, neither naturalists, nor ordinary people amongst us, could add up any kind of knowledge. There has to be a starting place. But the Creator provides that again and again – and so research can proceed. Water – left to itself – always runs downhill, never up; fire – left to itself – always burns, never freezes; day follows night – never fails; the tide goes out and in, unresting. I was immensely impressed to find how modern craftsmen had counted on God's dependability, in building, in one of Australia's cities, a tall War Memorial. Directed from an aperture they had made in its roof, was a tiny ray of light, falling on a central stone. Each year, for a measurable time, that ray, they knew, would fall one side of that stone, or off it in some other direction. But they built that great building on the understanding that *exactly at the eleventh hour, of the eleventh day, of the eleventh month each year*, when a Service of Sacred Remembrance took place therein, it would fall *dead central*. This couldn't have been planned in an erratic world, any more than could my daily newspaper include in its New Year issue a calendar of the tides in our beautiful Gulf, *for the whole year*! And it does this year after year for me. (Within this same world, a lot yet remains unknown, of course, about the laws that lie behind cyclones, earthquakes, and the like.)

Dr Paul Tillich, in our day, would have us understand : 'The starting point for natural Theology is not an argument, but *sharpened awareness*.' Unhappily, a number who hear this statement take fright at the word 'Theology'. That's a pity – they need not. (But for the sake of many readers of my books, through the years, I have deliberately sought to use simple words of our everyday life, rather than the theological terms in which I have had first to ponder their truth. And this book follows that pattern; though it always seems a loss not to quote occasionally from men and women with a specialized theological training. Theology, after all, only seeks to arrange in the neatest, richest order, fragments of knowledge about God and Man and Religion – and the growing relationship of each with the others.)

And religion, of course, is not a totally solemn matter – it is too human for that, beautiful sometimes, sometimes even hilarious. Laughter is one of the Creator's essential gifts, a kind of first-cousin to lively wit. Love, longing, and the practical expression of these in everyday life, know it. Secular and sacred strands are interwoven in it – and no one denomination has a monopoly of truth, light or love. Even hate finds a place in religion – following God's hatred of wrong, *though never of the wrongdoer*. The psalmist's statement of this was simple enough: *'Ye that love the Lord, hate evil'* (97:10). Catherine Booth was not by any means the only one who learned its relevance – though she learned it well. To the company gathered at her funeral service, her husband said this significant thing: 'She was good. She was a thorough hater of shams, hypocrisies, and make-believe . . . She was love!'

All this, all that is richest, and most practical in life, comes from God. But how are we to make our start to know Him? And where?

If men and women today don't find it as easy to begin with the world He has created, it may be that they have made it more difficult than it has ever been, by setting themselves far above it, in high-rise flats, like great bootboxes wherever we turn, in great sprawling cities, in every country that calls itself 'progressive'. Some speak of these modern-home-settings as 'concrete jungles', and psychiatrists grow solemn in telling us what they do for us as persons.

This is not surprising, when one thinks how cut off many of us are; how we never put our hands, or our feet, in the soil. Day after day, many, on rising, rush off to business, along made paths and roads, into cars, trains, buses – without ever so much as putting their feet on the earth itself. At day's end they return in the same manner – except for a break at holiday time – every single day of the working year; and every year of their working life.

This unnatural setting faced me first in London, before the war, but it has accelerated since, in other parts of the country, and in other countries. Token of its beginning is a stone I came across on the Goldsmith's Arms, in London's Elephant and Castle area. It did not strike me as ominous then. It said simply :

> Here Herbs did grow
> And Flowers sweet,
> And now 'tis called
> 'Saint George's Street'.

One might, all too aptly today, put up a similar plaque in many a place where things of the earth flourish no more.

Of course, public parks are valued – and many of them are beautiful. And there are in many crowded parts, cycling clubs, bird watching clubs, tramping clubs, camera clubs, and the like, to help men and women back to God's nature. Even to motor into the green countryside counts. A fisherman by his favourite stream is always ready to claim that he finds what he needs there – whatever the state of his actual catch – as much or more of God, he contends, than many another in church. And many a golfer claims as much for his links; whilst yet another praises the leisure he finds, bringing him to God, as he leans on a five-barred gate, or sits on a stile. Nature, of God's creating, is so wonderful! It can do so much for us, one by one.

But not enough! Many, familiar with Wordsworth's ramblings in the beautiful Lake District, where I came upon those three telling words under the tree, YOU ARE HERE!, or familiar with some of his poetry read at college, might be tempted to think otherwise. One has only to ponder the copy of a letter he wrote to Sir George Beaumont, to know that *he did not* derive from nature alone all that he needed to nourish his spirit – whatever it did for his body and mind. Said he: 'I look abroad upon Nature, *and I meditate upon the Scriptures* . . . and my creed rises up of itself with the ease of an exultation.' These two are meant to go together; Nature alone cannot lead one deeply enough.

As well as travelling, haversack on back, through the lovely parts known to Wordsworth, I have travelled amid the natural beauty of the tropical Pacific. There, despite its appeal, I have come across signs of the one-time ferocity of the brown man, and the even worse devilry of the white man, aided by his muskets and barter. Life was never safe in those parts, before the messengers of God came bearing those Scriptures that meant so much to Wordsworth, and to others loving Nature.

But bring what one finds in the Bible *to Nature*, and a wonderful knowledge of God can be possessed for life. I continually find myself using the Nature Prayer which Dr Walter Rauschenbush left permission for me to use:

O God, we thank Thee for this universe, our great home; for its vastness and its riches, and for the manifoldness of the life which teems upon it, and of which we are part. We praise Thee for the arching sky and the blessed winds, for the driving clouds and the constellations on high. We praise Thee for the salt sea and the running water, for the everlasting hills, for the trees, and for the grass under our feet. We thank Thee for our senses by which we can see the splendour of the morning . . . Grant us, we pray Thee, a heart wide open to all this joy and beauty, and save our souls from being so steeped in care or so darkened by passion that we pass heedless and unseeing when even the thorn-bush by the wayside is aflame with the Glory of God.

3. WHAT HAVE OTHERS TO TELL ME?

Keeping the flocks of his father-in-law, young Moses, on the back of the desert, certainly saw *God through Nature*. In the words of a modern speaker: 'It may have been only a thorn bush that Moses saw that day, a thorn bush aflame with blossoms, or a tree in the flaming colours of Autumn, or the sun shining on a patch of vegetation amid the desert sand. But God made it the means of revelation, so that the man was awed and solemnized; he felt that he was on holy ground, and listened for what God had to say.'

In the beautiful southern city where I was a student – Christchurch, New Zealand – I used often to go to a building standing in an avenue of great trees, almost always sun-flecked when I was free to visit it. It was the city's museum. But it was the beautiful words chiselled across its portico that attracted me to it first – words from Job, whom I have already quoted, in his search for God: '*Lo, these are parts of His ways*, but how little a portion is heard of Him.'

It would be hard to find a better, or more meaningful, sentence to prepare one's approach to that house of gathered treasures. The casual passer-by, or careful student, considering it, would have to acknowledge, however much he knew of what was within, that it was only *a part* of the revelation of God in this world. And it would still be true, if like young Moses confronted by the Burning Bush, he knew himself confronted, and felt moved to take the shoes from off his feet, because the ground whereon he stood was holy. (Exodus 3 : 1-6).

None of us – in a museum, or in the world of nature about us – can say: 'All of God is here!' He is so much more than any part of His creation. Though we may well marvel at His power that fastens the planets in their places; that fashions the tiniest seeds we know with mathematical exactness; that sends a babe out into this world, its tiny ten fingers fitted with pearly nails. I have remembered through years a day of which a nurse friend, now a tutor-sister, told me. For on that day she claimed, she met God, in the delivery-room of a nursing home. To see the perfection of a little life, and the clever manner of its coming into this world, was so wonderful, she knew it for an unmistakable sign of God's presence. 'I felt', said she, 'like taking the shoes from off my feet, there and then.'

But all of God was not, of course, to be known in any one of those expressions of Nature, wonderful as they might be. Of each of them one had, with Dryden the poet, to say :

> This is a piece too fair
> To be the child of Chance, and not of Care.
> No Atoms casually together hurl'd,
> Could e'er produce so beautiful a world !

But the God Whom we seek – and find often through nature – is more than creative power and grace. Little by little even Moses learned that later; and those who followed him as leader of the people during those early days of the race.

My mind turns to Amos, the prophet – a man with a country heart, a shepherd, from the small town of Tekoa. He saw that prosperity was limited to a few about him, and that it fed on the hard lives of the poor – for all that the time was counted a period of piety. In the middle of the eighth century before Christ, he raised his voice. His vision of God was of *a God of Justice.* With prosperity had grown the need for a rude awakening.

In time, came another: Hosea – a prophet out of the midst of domestic trouble, adding to Amos's idea of a God of Justice, *a God of Mercy.* All we know of this prophet is derived solely from the Old Testament book that bears his name. We see him as a man of great sensitivity. His wife, Gomer, had proved unfaithful, slipping off into the loose life of harlotry. It became an ugly story. But there was born within the heart of her suffering husband a desire to show mercy. So out into the sleazy streets he went to bring her back – saying, in effect : 'If

I, a man, can show this mercy, *how much more* must the Eternal Who made me, and stirred me to this attitude?' And this became the central truth of his prophecy: *the mercy of God!* So one revelation was added to another!

With the passing of time, *came yet another: Isaiah,* whose call to the service of God stands as one of the most exalted moments in the Old Testament. (Isaiah 6:1-8) 'In the year that King Uzziah died', it begins, 'I saw also the Lord sitting upon a throne, high and lifted up, and His train filled the temple. Above it stood the seraphims: each one had six wings; with twain he covered his face, and with twain he covered his feet, and with twain he did fly. And one cried unto another, and said, "Holy, holy, holy, is the Lord of hosts: the whole earth is full of His glory!" And the posts of the door moved at the voice of him that cried, and the house was filled with smoke. Then said I, "Woe is me! for I am undone; because I am a man of unclean lips, and I dwell in the midst of a people of unclean lips: for mine eyes have seen the King, the Lord of hosts!" Then flew one of the seraphims unto me, having a live coal in his hand, which he had taken with the tongs from off the altar; and he laid it upon my mouth, and said, "Lo, this hath touched thy lips; and thine iniquity is taken away, and thy sin purged." Also I heard the voice of the Lord, saying, "Whom shall I send, and who will go for us?" Then I said, "Here am I; send me!" '

From that moment, this young city man of Jerusalem was God's man, a leader among the people, and his emphasis was upon the *holiness of God.* A courtier, an aristocrat, his word was widely heard, for he was respected as a man of courage and of vision. The nations round about were, many of them, monsters of lust and cruelty. They had gods in plenty; they offered children as sacrifices; sexual display became a part of worship. But Isaiah's word about the holiness of God was unfaltering. At times, those addressed forgot – and suffered for their forgetting.

To this hour, Isaiah's message remains. In his fine book, *God and Man,* Dr Herbert Farmer says: 'We must keep the truth of *the Love of God,* and the truth of *the Holiness of God* . . . in quite inseparable connection with one an-other. We need to remind ourselves that when we say God is Love, we do mean God, the Holy One, high and lifted up, Whose thoughts are not as our thoughts, nor His ways as our ways.'

To these visions of God, others through the years have added : a *God of Purpose*; a *God of Beauty*. In our day, Dr Ralph Sockman says : 'Think of sunsets . . . We can calculate the exact moment of the sun's setting tomorrow or a year from tonight. But what can predict the colours of those sunsets? This evening the western sky may be adorned in gorgeous red; tomorrow night the garment may be purple flecked with gold. All that man's physical health would have required is the alteration of light and darkness. Yet the Creator throws in the sunset colours as extras.'

Some forms of beauty that God gives, of course, can be accounted for as contributing to necessity – the colour and fragrance of the flowers, designed to attract the bees and so secure fertilization. But this has been an over-worked theory from the start – it does not account for the beauty of the landscape, or for the beautiful forms of the clouds. And the theory breaks down altogether when one comes to forms of beauty that are unseen, for at the bottom of the sightless, lightless sea, and in the slimy, muddy lake bottom, are minute creatures so beautiful that, micro-scopically examined, they may be compared with the beauty of a rose window in a Gothic cathedral. Biological necessity cannot explain them. *'Why are these things so?'* *The answer*, Dr Herbert Farmer says, *'must be that God is a God of beauty – because He is a God Who loves what He has created.'*

I have watched a young mother, in the days of her patience, picking out with delicate touch the threads of a baby's tiny garment. I have seen her lovingly bending over her work, stitching a rose-bud here, and a spray of leaves there. Why? Will her unborn child know how beautiful this garment is? No! Will her child care, so long as it is warm and fed? No! Then why does she do it? Because she cannot help creating beauty – she is a lover. I look at the exquisite carving that some old monk has put on a seat-end in some obscure village church. The seat is no more comfortable because of it. Why does he do it? He does it, labouring painstakingly, because he is a lover. And it is of the nature of a lover to make something beautiful, something extra.

I look at this world – as prophets and psalmists and saints have looked at it – and I see everywhere in earth, sea and sky, beauty, the beauty of God. And words I read in the Book of Wisdom waken with significance: *'Never wouldst Thou have created anything, if Thou hadst hated it.'*

But I have to go further; for the greatest beauty of God's love is not in the wild flower of the embankment, the common beauty of the bursting bud, the unguessed symmetry where no man sees, the majesty of the skies – His greatest beauty is in the body, mind and spirit of man, *because His greatest love is centred there.*

'Whatever else God may be', says Professor Norman Pittenger, in *God's Way with Men*, 'He is One Who has with His human children relations that are more like those which we have with one another than they are like those which obtain between sticks and stones, between men and trees, or between dogs and cats. Furthermore, we say that *in Himself*, so far as we dare presume to speak of such a mystery, He is *more* like us in the kind of nature which is His, than He is like the nature which can be attributed to those sticks, stones, trees . . .'

We cannot be more practical than to accept God's personality, or go deeper than say of Him, as did Dr William Temple, so gloriously, in our day: 'When we deliberate, *He reigns*; when we decide wisely, *He reigns*; when we decide foolishly, *He reigns*; when we serve Him in humble loyalty, *He reigns*; when we serve Him self-assertively, *He reigns*!'

4. WHERE DOES THE GLORY OF GOD SHOW CLEAREST?

We have come, at this point, to think of God in terms of personality – this being the highest conception possible to us – and His relationship with us, as one of persons. (As Creator, He can't be less than the highest form of life He has created. So we have confidence to claim that it must be in this realm of reality that the answer we seek lies.)

Long ago, when the unknown writer of the New Testament book of Hebrews, toying with the same question, found himself able to answer as confidently, he used words that have never been forgotten : 'God, Who at sundry times, and in divers manners, spake in time past by the prophets, hath in these last days, spoken unto us by His Son, Whom He hath appointed heir of all things . . . *being the brightness of His glory, and the express image of His person!'* A magnificent statement, covering for us what we know as *The Incarnation*! In our day, T. S. Eliot strips it down to three simple lines :

> God so loved
> A small ball, spun
> On its own axis.

Such is our world, and the best-known verse in our New Testament concerns it (John 3 : 16), 'God so loved the world, that He gave His only begotten Son, that whosoever believeth in Him should not perish, but have everlasting Life.'

It came to me with rich meaning when first I walked along the Thames Embankment. For there, beside the path I took, I came upon the obelisk, Cleopatra's Needle, pointing upwards. It stood once in Heliopolis, capital of the ancient civilization. Then a time came when workmen dug it out of the sand, where it had collapsed, and towing it to London, prepared it for re-erection there. And to their surprise, they found a cavity at its heart. It contained children's toys as old as Moses, and metal mirrors of the ladies, and forms of adornment of the men of those early times. As these things were uncovered, it seemed to the workmen that they bore a message from the far-away past, to their own day. Soon, somebody suggested that before the old obelisk was re-sited, it should be filled up with modern toys, ladies' mirrors, men's razor-blades, and corresponding items – a message from our present to the future. And this was done. It sets me wondering what men of any future civilization, who chance to have dealings with them, will think of the things our civilization has sent forward. But of one item there – a single verse from the New Testament (John 3 : 16) – there can be no doubt. Copied in every language into which it was at that moment translated, it carried the world's greatest truth – that God had reached out in love to His people. Here, as nowhere else, shone the 'glory of God'.

Still Jesus is God's unique gift, His unique revelation, in this age when the footprints of fear are in all the earth. No less a speaker in our day than Dr J. Robert Oppenheimer, the atomic scientist, reminds us of the supreme wisdom of that revelation. Pleading for a liberation of funds for the exchange of students between countries, he says : 'The best way to send an idea is to wrap it up in a person.' He means that instead of turning over an abstract idea about Nigeria, let us live with a Nigerian student. There is a world of difference between the two, as I can bear witness after sharing life in a friend's home in Dublin with Addie, a young Nigerian medical student – coming to the same breakfast table each morning, and sharing in conversation around the fire at bed-time. Instead of thinking of Holland in the abstract, I have only to think of my friend Truus, and the day-to-day life we shared together - and the idea of Holland's life, her long-time history of oppression, her present triumph and enterprise, all light up in my teacher friend's bright face.

This, I know, is precisely what God did – this is the secret of the Incarnation. 'The Word became flesh', as St John says, 'and dwelt among us, *and we beheld His glory, the glory of the only begotten of the Father.*' The

love of God – for long waiting to be added to the revelation
of the prophets, Amos, Hosea, Isaiah, and others – was
now 'wrapped in a person'. Love was no longer a glory
in the heavens – it stretched out its hands as a babe in a
manger, born to two humble folk, attended by shepherds
straight from their work, smelling of the fields and sheep,
and later by kings, laden with rare gifts; it plays amidst
woodshavings beneath a carpenter's bench; it walks with
sandalled feet the dusty ways between village and village;
it reaches out tenderly to the leper, and to the distraught;
it blesses little children, and mothers with them; it flashes
with honest, kindly eyes, dividing the false from the true,
as men and women bring their problems, seeking help; it
clothes itself with rare authority, whipping animals out of
the Temple; it restores Mary Magdalene to the dignity
of womanhood; it pushes out with fishermen on their all-
night tasks; it kneels after sundown in an Upper Room,
to wash disciples' feet. Imagine it! God a man, moving
among men and women, talking in language that reaches
hearts – about God, and about the length to which His
love will go. Then going that length, past arrest, false
judgement, to a Cross on a stark hill outside a city wall;
winning through to triumph in a garden, with a stone
rolled away from a tomb. So Jesus rises from the dead,
to be alive for ever more! This is the Incarnation – God's
ultimate earth-revealing of Himself – a wonderful reality
'wrapped in human form'. Men and women have been
trying to put it in their own words ever since – but how
poorly they succeed. One says :

> I know not how that Bethlehem's Babe
>   Could in the God-head be;
> I only know the Manger Child
>   Has brought God's Love to me.

> I know not how that Joseph's tomb
>   Could solve Death's mystery :
> I only know a living Christ,
>   Our immortality.

As Dr Emil Brunner, one of our century's great scholars, says : *'It is the fact of the Incarnation, and not its mode, that matters.'* There is still controversy in some quarters about *how* His life began – what we call 'The Virgin Birth' – so that many feel it cannot be made an article of faith. But many Christians believe it, despite the silence among the greater part of New Testament scribes – perhaps out of gentle consideration for Mary, still living when a number of them were writing. What little they could do, they did, to save scandal from settling on her shoulders. The Apostles' Creed – not, of course, compiled by the first apostles – speaks clearly of : 'Jesus Christ His only Son our Lord, Who was conceived by the Holy Ghost, Born of the Virgin Mary, Suffered under Pontius Pilot, Was crucified, dead, and buried. He descended into hell; The third day He rose again from the dead; He ascended into heaven, And sitteth on the right hand of God the Father Almighty. From thence He shall come to judge the quick and the dead.' It is impossible to hold any claim greater than these words carry.

One might fail to find God in Nature, or even in the words of the prophets, but Bethlehem brought a new factor. I have walked in that little land where it became reality. But all over the world it is celebrated at Christmas year by year, still. Spangles, stars, gifts, crackers and cards come to the fore then. But Christmas is more than all of these – it's not alone a festival for children – but *the Birthday of One Child* !

It's not a piece of folk-lore – though it gathers all sorts of happenings around it. The children of Geneva are better served in this than ours – or any others I know the world round. They have *two* festivals in December : one on the second of the month, the other, the one we treasure, on the 25th. If you chance to be in Geneva for the earlier festival, you are not likely to forget it. All the sweet-shops at that time are filled with little chocolate cooking-pots. This is a feature of *The Escalade*, and goes back to 1602, when the city was surprisingly delivered from an attempt on it by the Duke of Savoy and his soldiers. An old grandmother, busy at her stove, heard the tramp of armed men approaching, and looking out saw that they were not far off, and would pass beneath her high window. In an instant she knew what she would do – and in the next, did it! She lifted her large iron cooking-pot with its contents, off the fire, and hurled it down through her open window, into the street just ahead of the on-coming soldiers. The surprised Savoyards broke ranks, and the story I heard in Geneva says the city was saved!

(Being one of those awkward people, a writer, my first question was: 'Is that true?' My Swiss acquaintance stood first on one leg, and then on the other, and ended with the words: 'Well, does it matter? The children love the little cooking-pots.')

Nevertheless, there is a vast difference between *fact* and *folk-lore*. Professor C. H. Dodd leaves us with no doubt about this. Says he: 'Some religions can be indifferent to historical fact, and move entirely upon the plane of timeless truth. Christianity cannot. It rests upon the affirmation that a series of events happened, in which God revealed Himself in action, for the salvation of men.' This can't be too clearly seen. The festival that we hold on 25 December is not a piece of folk-lore. A clear line is drawn, purposefully and unforgettably, in the New Testament records (Luke 2 : 1-14). Who would not be impressed with its detailed verification? 'In those days, there went out a decree from Caesar Augustus, that all the world should be taxed. [It was their known world, their little world; but in every sense, concerned.] And the taxing was first made when Cyrenius was governor of Syria.' There were, thereabouts, numbers living who could check it, as if one might say of an event in our day: 'It happened when Queen Elizabeth, our beloved, celebrated her Silver Jubilee.' As real as that! An historical happening! Luke's record adds other details that might be verified: 'All went to be taxed . . . and Joseph also went up from Galilee, out of the city of Nazareth, into Judea, unto the city of David, which is called Bethlehem; because he was of the house and lineage of David.' (One could check every place.) The chief characters are this craftsman, and a village girl, Mary, with a remarkable story to hold in her heart. To them, in Bethlehem, that census-time, *a child is born*! And He is none other than One spoken of by the prophets, as 'the Son of God!' 'When the fullness of Time was come' – as my favourite New Testament verse says – 'God sent forth His Son, made of a woman . . . to redeem.' (Galatians 4 :4 & 5).

It happened, says a modern poet :

> In a crowded public house, in occupied
>   territory
> where there was no room for anybody
>   extra
> and rations were scanty . . .

As I read between the lines, I'm sure it was harsher than many imagine. Nazareth, on the hills, was a little place of no consequence – nobody of any importance ever came from there – and Bethlehem that night was over-crowded. True, the young woman was plainly soon to have a baby, but what of that? Women had been having babies since the beginning of time. It was hard to turn the couple away, but what could a harassed inn-keeper do? Somebody had to sleep out with the animals that night. The place was pestered with querulous travellers, sharing hate for the census, a universal reaction to levied taxes. To add to it, this couple was without influence – the simple stark truth was, 'There was no room in the Inn'.

We moderns have tricked up the scene in starry tinsel, for the sake of shopkeepers and children, whose main celebration of the year it is. Before ever I went to little Bethlehem, walked its streets, and visited the site where He was born and laid in a manger, it was Mrs Slater, writing from the south of England, who helped me to understand what it must have been like. In a letter, she re-told : 'As our first Christmas in the Shanghai Intern-ment Camp drew near, "the days were fulfilled" when we should have our first little one. I was not allowed to go to hospital, and so, as the first warning became evident, the splendid team-work which camp-life produced, was set in motion.

'Thank God, the missionary doctor and nurse, in the midst of the daily anxieties of keeping the camp healthy, were equal to this sudden situation. A small room was hastily cleared, a table moved in, and the cleaning squad washed the walls as high as they could reach. As I lay on the table, I could see the wavy line along the wall which marked the height of their endeavours.

'There were no instruments, no anaesthetics, and but the simplest of drugs; nothing for an emergency. But God was good. Soon there was a cry of a man-child born into the world.

'Resting in bed, I could not attend the roll-call next morning, so the Japanese guard came to my bedside to see if I was really there. As he counted one extra little internee, even he smiled. Then came some of our fellow-internees to see the little mite, bringing gifts from their own meagre store – little garments outgrown by others, useful towels, bits of sheeting for nappies. The gifts of the Wise Men could not have meant more to Mary than those gifts did to me. There were none of the usual things so often thought necessary for a Happy Christmas, not even freedom to come and go; but as Christmas Day dawned, it was with the deepest sense of happiness that my husband and I looked into the home-made canvas cot of our first little son. Did Mary and Joseph feel like that, I asked, that first Christmas morning?'

It was something like that, when God's own Son was born – fashioned of atoms, sensitively clothed in man's five senses, to open His eyes on earth, and be suckled by a young mother – *an historical happening.*

But there was something different from every other birth in time, at Bethlehem. For this little one born, *both human and divine,* grew to be a person with knowing, feeling, willing, as the term implies – but without sin, or any sense of guilt. He was not just 'a good man'. Every good man whom we know, has a sense of guilt – the better the man he is, the keener. It is at this point that the uniqueness of Jesus emerges gloriously. He spoke of this Himself – and no man argued back. This struck me as truly remarkable when first I faced it clearly. For of all

35

men, those disciples of His might well have been the first
to speak up. From earliest childhood they had been trained
that *God was One* – now here was one claiming to be
one with God! Publicly, they heard Him challenge:
'Which of you convicteth Me of sin?' None spoke up. He
lived closely with His men, so that no human fault could
be hidden – travelling, involved with pressing crowds,
camping out-of-doors; growing thirsty so that He had to
beg a drink at a well; at night so weary that He fell
asleep in the end of Peter's little boat on the lake. So
human was He! At the same time, He lived so closely
with His Father. *And the holiness of God did not rebuke
Him.*

To those disciples – under those conditions – He could
say: 'Believe Me that I am in the Father, and the Father
in Me; or else believe Me for the very work's sake' (John
14:11). When one of that close little company asked Him:
'Show us the Father', His answer, without hesitancy, was:
'Have I been so long time with you, and yet thou hast not
known Me, Philip? *He that hath seen Me hath seen the
Father*' – in modern speech: *What I am in time, that God
is eternally.*

He is 'God, coming out of the inaccessible distances, and
drawing indescribably near.' Human, and Divine!

But there is one lastingly important reality here, underlined for us today by Dr J. B. Phillips, in *Your God is Too
Small*: 'It would be a mistake to suppose that the Eternal
God is no "bigger" than Jesus of Nazareth, limited as He
was by time and space and circumstance. *But the biggest,
widest and highest ideas of God that mind can conceive
arrange themselves without dissonance or incongruity
around the character Jesus revealed.*'

Ever since Christianity has offered room for close
thought and critical questioning; but at the end, Jesus
still stands supreme. Under every test He shows Himself
to be what He claimed to be – *both human and divine.*
Unlike any other faith, Christianity stands, based – not on
folk-lore, but on historical fact – *on the unique person of
Jesus Christ.* ('Confucianism', as Dr Murdo Macdonald
reminds us from Edinburgh, 'is a collection of ethical

maxims. Mohammedanism is a religion of a book rigidly interpreted and absolutely binding on its devotees. Christianity is the religion, not of a book but *of a person*. Jesus commissioned His Apostles and established His Church before there were any written records of His earthly ministry. Christians in the last resort are asked to give their allegiance – not to any dogma or abstract article of belief, but to *the Living Lord, the Risen Christ*, Who still speaks and communes with His believing people.')

5. WHAT OF ALL THOSE SAD PICTURES?

Medieval artists, and many relatively modern, have shown us Jesus with a sad face, with seemingly no reckoning on His joy.

When I turn to the New Testament, I find the words 'Joy', and 'great Joy', no less than fifty-three times. This makes it the most joyous religious book in the world. It opens with joy over the birth of Jesus, and ends with the magnificent word-picture of a multitude which no man could number, rejoicing.

Clearly, if the corners of our mouths are continually down, something is amiss with our Christianity.

This is not to make little of the fact that upon this earth our Lord was called 'The Man of Sorrows'. Unhappily, for many in our midst He still carries no other title. But He was also 'The Man of Joy'. And it was no ordinary joy, at the mercy of things that could happen. It was something also more than *jollity*, which can be an evanescent thing, momentarily bubbling up, soon gone.

Twice a week – on Mondays and Thursdays in New Testament times – the Pharisees fasted. Often it was a forced, insincere abstinence. At that time, the Law always exempted a bridal party from fasting. But it must have greatly surprised those who listened to Jesus, moving in the midst of His disciples, to hear Him say : 'We are as a bridal-party !'

Lately, I went back to one of our big city churches – Pitt Street Methodist – to speak. With pleasure, I found myself recalling a country-wide conference of ministers and lay representatives I once attended there. Someone was addressing the Chair, on that occasion, as I became aware that sitting next to me was a small boy – a very small boy with a dirty face, and a piece of chewing-gum. He was pulling it in and out, making fantastic patterns with it. There was no other child in that august company.

Soon, the little fellow whispered, 'Isn't the organ going

to play?' 'No, no, not today,' I was obliged to answer. 'Then I'd better be going,' he whispered, and with that, slipped out.

Later, when we came out of conference, a friend on the other side of me, a teacher of music, said : 'I'm sure that little fellow was one of three who came here in the holidays. I was deputizing for the organist; and one afternoon, as I was practising here, I heard children's voices. I turned on my stool, and three of them were standing inside the church. I called : "You mustn't play in here; this is the church." One of them answered : "Oh, we came to hear the organ." "Well, if that is what you want, you'd better come up here, and see it as well," I said, "and all its wonderful stops and keys." At such close range', said my friend, 'they were speechless. Then, the little one of the trio - about seven – looked up beseechingly, with : "Miss, could you play 'Here comes the bride'?" '

'And what did you do?' I asked. 'I played it for her,' said my friend, 'I played it for her childish joy – "*Here comes the bride*".'

Her reply delighted me – I was so sure it would delight our Master. He spoke of little children of His day playing weddings in the market-place; and as I stuffed my conference-agenda into my bag at day's end, I stepped off lightly.

I recalled that the Master's first miracle was performed at a wedding in Cana. Preparations for it, of course, had been made long before dusk. Suddenly, music was in the air, along with the flashing of tiny lamps. All the village was out in the street to watch the procession. First came the musicians, playing sweet airs upon their flutes; then came girls carrying poles with lighted lamps; after them appeared the little bride, and lastly, the bridegroom and his friends in their best and gayest clothes.

Soon the procession reached the bridegroom's house – decorated and lighted for the occasion – and all went in. Soon the feast began. Jesus was among the guests – pleased to be present, and wanted for Himself, not just as a pious person seizing the opportunity to 'speak a good word in season'. Joy was such an essential of His personality, that

Christianity Close to Life

He fitted well into a wedding feast – the greatest moment in the lives of two young folk. He was so different from so many religious leaders. And He did not send an excuse. I felt certain He would be glad to hear a little child look up expectantly, with: 'Miss, could you play, "Here comes the bride"?'

His immediate fore-runner, John the Baptist – not to mention other prophets and teachers who had preceded Him - wouldn't easily have accepted an invitation to a wedding. Jesus's approachability, and His joy, led some who looked on to question His credentials as a teacher. They said: 'He eats and drinks'; 'He mixes with doubtful characters'. Of course, He was young; He was just setting out on His life-work; He was surrounded by friends. But the true source of His joy lay deeper than any of these things – *there was His supreme trust in the character of God. He believed He knew His will, and was doing it. He believed that love, chief of God's eternal values, would come right in the end, whatever happened!*

The evil and anguish of the Cross lay no distance ahead when Jesus gathered with His friends for *a last supper*, this time, in an Upper Room. He made no attempt to avoid talk on what might well lie ahead – though it was painful talk. 'These things have I spoken unto you', said He to those about Him, 'that *My joy* may be in you, and that *your joy* may be fulfilled' (John 15:11). And again: 'Ye therefore now have sorrow; but I will see you again, and your heart shall rejoice, and your joy no one taketh away from you' (John 16:22).

There was not much time between that *first feast* – a wedding-feast of a bride and bridegroom in Cana – and that *last feast* – a meal with His disciples, before the crisis of the Cross.

Nor did His joy end there. When the Crucifixion was over, and the Resurrection, and the Ascension had become a reality, we read of those same disciples and their friends: 'They returned to Jerusalem *with great joy.*' They might have returned from such a parting with unrestrained sorrowing – they did not. They believed – and confirmed it in experience – that physical separation had no power to shatter the joy they had from Him. And sure of Him, and sure of God, in Whom He trusted, they moved on. His words to them had been : '*Lo, I am with you always,* even unto the end of the world!' (Matthew 28 :20). So His seen presence became His unseen presence!

Times were different in many ways, but not easier than any we know now. In Dr J. B. Phillips's words : 'The Christian faith took root and flourished in an atmosphere almost entirely pagan, where cruelty and sexual immorality were taken for granted, where slavery and inferiority of women were almost universal, while superstition and rival religions with all kinds of bogus claims existed on every hand. Within this pagan chaos the early Christians, by the power of God within them, lived lives as sons of God, demonstrating purity and honesty, patience and genuine love. They were pioneers of the new humanity.' They possessed the joy of Christ!

And all down the long centuries since – whatever the untoward circumstances – men and women have been kept by this good gift from being sullen saints. St Bernard of Clairvaux found simple words to remind himself and his fellows of this glorious reality :

> *Jesu, thou joy of loving hearts,*
>   Thou Fount of Life, Thou Light of men,
> From the best bliss that earth imparts,
>   We turn unfilled to Thee again.

In our day, we know still the deep source of Joy that Jesus shared with the first disciples : the dependable character of God; the confidence St Bernard and his friends knew in the unfailing adequacy of His love; the interpretation of that love by loved friends and family this moment close to our lives; the discovery that, embraced deeply, this Joy is unending!

6. DOES THE WORD 'MEEK' MEAN 'WEAK'?

Words one is taught to lisp in childhood can often create problems later on. The word 'meek' became a bother to me. I met it in my first prayer :

> Gentle Jesus, *meek* and mild,
> Look upon a little child . . .

I don't know whether little children are taught it today — I rather hope not. Happily, today, religious bookshops have little paperbound books of prayers of a more suitable kind. Our parents could do nothing better than they did : faithfully pass on this tiny prayer with the word 'meek', that had been taught them too in childhood.

As part of our grown-up picture of Jesus (following on our chapter about His joy) I want to spend a little space on this word. (Each chapter of this book, as you will have discovered by now, is a whole in itself; though each belongs to a sequence of questions that claims an answer in one's on-going Christian life.)

Apart from bed-time prayer, I sometimes heard the word 'meek' linked to the word 'little', to describe a wordless fellow who biked past our country home most days to go to work at the nearby mill. In his relationship with his fellows, he was a very incapable person. 'Meek little Claudie', suited him well; and I was all but grown-up before I shook that unhappy connotation from the word 'meek'. Nobody in person, or in any book I read at that time, thought to explain to me the meaning of that word that had become such a bother. *'Blessed are the meek'*, I read in my New Testament. But I didn't want to be among the blessed — my thoughts were immediately of little Claudie. Further on, in the same Gospel of Matthew, I came upon another saying of our Lord, which added to my puzzlement. There was a mistake somewhere. He said, according to Matthew, *'I am meek and lowly in heart*' (11 : 29).

Then, one day, light fell like a shaft of sunlight across this problem. I chanced on Dr Harry Fosdick's little book, *The Manhood of the Master*. It was already in its seventh edition, and had helped many a one like myself, growing into knowledge of God, through Christ. Its twelve thoughtful chapters spoke of 'The Master's Joy . . . Magnanimity . . . Indignation . . . Loyalty . . . Endurance . . . Sincerity . . . Self-restraint . . . Fearlessness . . . Affection . . . Scale of Values . . . Spirit', and ended with a splendid summing-up, 'The Fulness of Christ'. By this time I was ready to agree with Dr Fosdick – and thankful that I could. Said he : 'We have been compelled to notice *the remarkable poise* in which our Master holds opposing virtues, that with us are most difficult of combination.' (And with this, we were at the heart of the secret of 'meekness'.)

My repeated reading and study of the Gospels since, has led me to confirm that Jesus was anything but 'weak', in the dictionary sense. Bernard Shaw, in his characteristic forthrightness, said as much : ' "Gentle Jesus, *meek* and mild" is a snivelling modern invention, with no warrant in the Gospels.' If you would welcome confirmation of this by a New Testament scholar, I can't introduce you to anyone better than my good friend, Dr William Barclay. He had the original Greek at his finger-tips, and the happy knack of being able to express profundities in clear, simple English that we can all understand. Many of us have read his paperback *Daily Study Notes on the New Testament*; and have seen and heard him on television, if not in the pulpit or in the lecture room.

'In our modern English idiom', he admits, 'the word *meek* is hardly one of the honourable words of life. It carries with it the idea of spinelessness, and subservience, and mean-spiritedness. It paints the picture of a submissive and ineffective creature. But it so happens that the word *meek* – in Greek, *praus* – was one of the great Greek ethical words. It was Aristotle's fixed method to define every virtue as *the mean between two extremes.* On the one hand, there was the extreme of excess; on the other hand, there was the extreme of defect; and *in between* there

43

was the virtue itself, the happy medium. (To take an example – on the one extreme there is the spend-thrift; on the other there is the miser; and *in between* there is the generous man.)'

The word *praus* had a second standard Greek usage. It is the regular word for an animal which has become domesticated, which has been trained to obey the word of command, which has learned to answer to the reins. So the second possible translation is : *'Blessed is the man who has every instinct, every passion under control. Blessed is the man who is entirely self-controlled.'* This is a rendering more easily understood than that of the Authorized Version, on which many of us grew up : 'Blessed are the *meek*, for they shall inherit the earth.' (Matthew 5 : 5). When one understands the true meaning of the word rendered *meek*, it has about it a sense of splendid control and is wholly strong and admirable. And nothing seems more right than to describe our Master as 'meek'. In the French translation of the New Testament, we get the lovely, strong word of balance, *débonnaire* – and it has something for us that *meek* does not hold.

Paul speaks of the 'meekness and gentleness of Christ' (2 Corinthians 10 : 1). The suggestion that *meekness* was *weakness* never entered his head. He knew the word in all its splendid balance : the quality of a man who acts with gentleness while he has the power to act with sternness. *Meekness,* in its truest sense, is a rare mastery – no sudden situation ever shook our Master's poise. Even when men lauded Him – having eaten of His loaves and fishes – He kept His head. Even when they tore down palm branches and cried 'Hosanna!' as He rode into Jerusalem – He remained serene. Even when they brought Him up for judgement, and with loud cries lashed Him – He kept His dignity.

The Greeks asserted their pride of language; the Jews their pride of race; the Romans their pride of power – but here was something different. The conduct of this *meek* man, Jesus – even in this dark hour – was not one of shrinking into weak self-pity. So that when the women on the edge of the crowd showed their tears, His words to them were : 'Daughters of Jerusalem, weep not for Me, but weep for yourselves, and for your children.' (Luke 23 : 28). When the dastardly deeds of men neared their end, and on the Cross He breathed His last, hoisted high, one of the centurions suddenly found his tongue, to say, as one deeply moved : *'Truly, this man was the Son of God!'*

There is, to our loss, no single English word that precisely expresses the quality of balance at the back of that word we translate *meek*. Meekness is therefore a most misunderstood word. No wonder it took me years to evaluate it, as it appears in the first tiny prayer to cross my lips, and in the New Testament.

'The renewal of the earth', said Dietrich Bonhoeffer, the young Christian who gave his life for his faith in the concentration camp, 'begins at Golgotha, where the *meek* one died.'

Following on came the glory of the Resurrection, the Ascension, and the lasting promise of His presence with us ever more. Meekness, we see in Him superbly, is *strength held in restraint.*

7. JESUS'S QUESTION IS 'DO YOU BELIEVE NOW?'

One's childhood faith matters, of course – with its lively wonders; one's adolescent search, with its growing conception of God; but just now, it is the beauty of *now*, with its ever-growing reality of God, and human relationships, which matters most to me.

'*Now*', wrote St Paul, 'is the accepted time, behold *now* is the day of salvation.' Again, '*Now* are ye full, *now* are ye rich.' To these gloriously confident assertions, he added: 'The life which I *now* live in the flesh, I live by faith in the Son of God, Who loved me, and gave Himself for me.' (II Corinthians 6:2; I Corinthians 4:8, Galatians 2:20).

> Think not the Faith by which the just shall live
>   Is a dead creed, a map correct of heaven,
> Far less a feeling, fond and fugitive,
>   A thoughtless gift, withdrawn as soon as given;
> *It is an affirmation and an act*
> *That bids eternal truth be present fact!*
>
> Coleridge

The past offers meaning to us only because it was God's past – and led to *now*; the future offers challenge, only because it is God's future, and springs from *now*!

Jesus's question addressed to His disciples about Him, was, 'Do you *now* believe?' (John 16:31). He was not concerned, at that point, with the past or with the future, it was *now* that mattered most.

When skies are blue, sweet assurance breathes easily, but a crisis situation, as we all know, asks for a certainty that goes deeper. In church, it is easy enough to affirm 'I believe', using perhaps, the ancient words of the Apostles' Creed. Others, up through the years, have found other words to say as much. Cardinal Newman's phrase: 'Firmly I believe and truly', has a glorious ring, which has led me to make use of it again and again, to match my own experience. Pressures reach up sometimes from the past, and weaknesses of the present intrude – and it's not always easy to believe. In his *Credo*, of this century, poet Richard Watson Gilder speaks for many a one of us:

> How easily my neighbour chants his Creed,
> Kneeling beside me in the House of God.
> His 'I believe', and 'I believe',
> With cheerful iteration and consent –
> Watching meantime the white, slow sunbeam move
> Across the aisle, or listening to the bird
> Whose free, wild song sounds through the open door.
>
> Thou God supreme – I, too, believe!
> But oh! forgive if this one human word,
> Binding the deep and breathless thought of Thee
> And my own conscience with an iron band,
> Stick in my throat. I cannot say it, thus –
> This 'I believe!'

Belief that matters, of course, is in the present tense – like breathing, it is a matter of *now*. I like the way Lilian McDonald, Headmistress of Park School, Glasgow, puts it. 'If I were standing on a mountain-top or by an open sea assailed by all the winds of heaven, and were asked: "Why are you breathing?" what should I say? I should say that I cannot but do so; my lungs are made *to inhale air or die*. This air and I are part of the complex pattern of life, each smallest part of which has its own essential place in the pattern. When asked *why I believe in God*, I must make a like reply. I am assailed – my mind, my soul, whatever you call the essential me – at all points inescapably by the Creator. I see Him in the movement of the spheres; I see Him in the amusing efficiency of the hind legs of a honey bee; I see Him in the lives of men and in history. I feel His presence, on rare occasions so palpable as to be like a hand laid on the shoulder and a word spoken in the ear. I know that I am to live by His life and to be part of His mighty pattern. I cannot remember a time when I did not believe, so that I have no dramatic spiritual experience to relate. As a child, I accepted the quiet faith of my parents. I was well-instructed in church, home and school. This is not *sufficient reason* for belief', she finishes. 'I know that some, having started in this way, have departed from it.' That is true; many drop their childish faith, as ineffective – *there is no 'now' in it*. Belief has never been, to many such, more real than 'pins-and-needles in the knees', as they sat listening to Bible stories; it has never taken hold of all-important knowing, feeling, willing at the centre of personality. Even the early habits of story-telling, Sunday-school-going, church-going are dropped – in their place doubts and dull arguments show their heads. Exacting relationships push in; newspaper headlines about natural disasters, confuse; and life gets filled up with other absorbing things. They never reach the place where individually, with the consent of all one's faculties, it is possible to say, 'I believe!' And 'Now!'

One can't live joyously, colourfully, triumphantly, on what God did yesterday – in childhood, in youth, or before one reached middle-aged tiredness. And it is an irreparable loss if ever the pages of the Gospels grow meaningless or tame. 'These are written', said John plainly, *'that you may believe* that Jesus is the Christ, the Son of God, and that believing, you may have life in His name.' (John 20 : 31).

Belief is meant to fill all one's life – and now; life is meant to be a practical thing – now!

Of the countless books I have read on the earth-life of Jesus – and many of the beautiful books on His mysticism, His mastery in prayer, His magnanimity – I have never yet read one on His practicality. Yet, was any leader more practical? He grew up, of course, in a craftsman's family; He wore garments that had been patched by His mother's deft fingers – or where else did He get His knowledge of the futility of putting new patches on to old fabric? He earned His bread, and that of His widowed mother and the rest of the growing family still dependent, when Joseph died. He worked at a craftsman's bench, making things of the everyday – stools, yokes – and mending things for the many who couldn't afford to buy new. In those days the work of a carpenter entailed more than the careful use of prepared timbers; from the moment a forest tree was felled, it became his responsibility.

And when the time came to put up the shutters of that little workshop, and to enter upon what we persist in calling His 'public ministry', He was still *the practical man*. The same sure eye and hand that made it possible to turn out a good plough-beam, or a finely-fitting lid on a chest where moths intent on getting in would be defeated, took pains to seat the hungry multitude in fifties and sixties on the green grass when He fed them. So practical! I am indebted to missionary Timothy Richard of China for this observation. In his diary, he set down what to him had great worth: 'In the course of morning worship, I read the passage about our Lord feeding the multitudes, *where He made them sit down*. Like a flash of lightning the secret of sitting down was revealed. A sitting crowd cannot crush . . .'

Again, see Him in the home of Jairus, when his little girl was at death's door. Hindered on His way by crowds and a sick woman seeking to touch His garments without being seen, Jesus was unable to reach the ruler's house before those there believed the little girl to be dead. Taking with Him the distressed parents, and but three of His close friends, He entered, to take her hand, and speak softly: *Talitha cumi* – 'Little one, I say unto thee, arise!' And straightaway, she arose, and walked; for she was of the age of twelve. 'And he charged them' Mark says, 'that no one should know it' and – here comes a strikingly practical word – '*He commanded that something should be given her to eat.*' So practical!

The same spirit marks His campaigning. He knows men's reactions in crowds – so easily swayed by the emotion of the moment. He will have no follower regret his action on the morrow, or when he meets the difficulties entailed. No! Let him now count the cost!

To match another situation He tells of an impractical builder: 'Which of you, intending to build a tower, sitteth not down first, and counteth the cost, whether he hath sufficient to finish it? Lest haply, after he hath laid the foundation, and is not able to finish it, all that behold it begin to mock him, saying, "This man began to build, and was not able to finish." '

Nor did death change His practicality. One instance will suffice. Cast down by the events of the Crucifixion, the disciples had taken Peter's lead, and gone fishing. But fish were scarce, and they came home in the early morning, tired, with empty boats. On the shore one stood to greet them. 'And as soon as they were come to land, *they saw a fire of coals there, and fish laid thereon, and bread.*' This was the kindly provision of a practical man – that same man with Whom they had companied, teaching, praying, healing, quickening into new significance ordinary affairs of everyday life. Jesus Christ !

And this, in the mercy of God, is the one with Whom we have to do ! M. Clemenceau, the French statesman, knew well what his words meant when, speaking at a great conference, he said : 'I like talking to Colonel House, *because he is so practical. The President talks like Jesus Christ!*'

8. WHAT HAS CHRIST'S CROSS TO DO WITH ME?

It happened two thousand years ago, in another country, and I wasn't born.

'One of the most solemn facts in all history – one of the most significant for anybody who cares to ponder over it', said Herbert Butterfield, Professor of Modern History at the University of Cambridge, 'is the fact that Jesus Christ was not merely murdered by hooligans in a country road; He was condemned by everything that was respectable in that day, everything that pretended to be most righteous – the religious leaders of the time, the authority of the Roman government, and even the democracy itself which shouted to save Barabbas rather than Christ . . . In a profound sense we may say that the Crucifixion, however else we may interpret it, accuses human nature, accuses all of us in the very things that we think are our righteousness.'

The death of Socrates, scholars claim, succeeded in stopping 'the moral rot' in ancient Athens, by the example of a good man who chose death rather than betray his principles. But Christians hold more than this about the death of Christ. We speak about it in different terms. But only in recent years have I come upon Principal Charles Duthie – sharing with me the writing of a page in *The British Weekly* – saying : 'None of them completely satisfies.' And pondering the issue, I find I have to agree. Dean Matthews of St Paul's, adds : 'We need to get clear on the point that *no one doctrine of the Atonement* is part of the Christian faith, and that many different views are possible concerning the manner of Divine Forgiveness.'

A mystery so great, touching so many of us up through the centuries, is not simply stated. Some, indeed, even believe that it could not be counted just that one should bear the sins of many. But even in human relationships, we are bound to each other in innumerable ways; and we believe, on the authority of Jesus, that God the Father, and His Son Himself, are more wonderfully *one* (John

14 : 10). Might it not then be that the suffering, and the triumph of either, is the suffering and triumph of both? More than that – we are assured, in Christ's own words – that His going to the Cross, was entirely voluntary (John 10 : 18).

Others, yet again, dare believe that if one bear the sins of many, many might be thereby encouraged to sin *with impunity*. Their mood Paul set down in unforgettable words : 'Shall we continue to sin, that grace the more abound?' (Romans 6 : 1). This is a very base argument. If God forgives freely, surely He expects more than this – surely He counts on men confessing sins, and departing from the repetition of them.

You will not find it tedious, I hope, if I pause a moment, to state here a number of the theories of what was done on the Cross.

The *first* claim is that the merit of Jesus's offering lay in *His obedience*. Not only was this shown in His brief life, but in His dying, which somehow made it possible for God the Father to offer forgiveness to His sinful earth-children. Those who hold with unquestioning faith to this theory of the Atonement, slip in Scripture words about Christ 'becoming *obedient*, even unto death, yea, the death of the Cross.' (Philippians 2 : 8).

A second theory seems to owe an early origin to remembrance of the slave market, for it lays its emphasis upon an accepted deal, affecting men and women. This is no longer a general practice in our community, fortunately. But those who look back to the early days, when such transactions were commonplace, find in it an explanation of what Christ did on the Cross. 'The Son of Man', they quote, 'came not to be ministered unto, but to minister, and to give His life *a ransom for many*.' (Mark 10 : 45). And again : 'We are redeemed, not with corruptible things, with silver and gold . . . but with precious blood . . . even the blood of Christ.' (I Peter 1 : 18-19).

And there are others, *thirdly*, who approach it through the familiar Old Testament practice of *sacrifice*, effective in itself. They use the word 'propitiation' – though it puzzles some who, unsure of it, find, in consulting their

dictionary, that it means 'buying off an offended person'.
And this creates problems. Dr Leslie Weatherhead is not
alone in confessing that when a certain form of Communion service is used, where the word 'propitiation' waits
to be repeated, he feels uneasy. I can understand that.
How can one fit into it the idea of *God the Father*, that
Jesus gave to us? 'But', they hasten to add, 'the word
appears in Scripture: "If any man sin, we have an
advocate with the Father, Jesus Christ the righteous:
and He is the *propitiation* for our sins: and not for ours
only, but also for the sins of the whole world".' (I John
2 : 2). But what can we say of this shedding of blood? It
was easy for those steeped in Judaism to carry forward
these word-pictures, in their efforts to explain the Cross.
'For if the blood of goats and bulls, and the ashes of a
heifer', argued the unknown writer of the New Testament
book of Hebrews, 'sprinkling them that have been defiled,
sanctify unto the cleanness of the flesh: how much more
shall the blood of Christ, Who through the eternal Spirit
offered Himself without blemish unto God, cleanse our
conscience from dead works to serve the living God.'
(Hebrews 9 : 13-14). But what can a modern disciple make
of these words? To some of us they are repugnant – and
not easy to sing, as did our fathers and mothers, one by
one :

> Wash me in the blood of the Lamb,
> And I shall be whiter than snow,

any more than to sing :

> Exacted is the legal pain.

Fourthly, we must acknowledge the faith of those who
believe, above all else, that the Cross had power, as representing *the curse of condemnation*. Christ came up against
the Law, these claim, and against all that it represented
in politics, religion, and community. In so doing, He
showed once and for all how deeply ingrained is sin.
'Curseth', they repeat, 'is every one that hangeth on a

tree.' (Galatians 3 : 13). But surely, when the depth of sin is seen by each sinner, something more is needed to wrench him from its hold, and its outcome.

It is the fifth way of approach to the Cross that has meaning for most of us today. It is not centred on any legal, market, or sacrificial transaction – because we have no answer to the awkward query: 'To whom is the sacrifice made, the redeeming price paid?' When some answer: 'The Devil', it seems that language, and the use of these word-pictures, fails. It seems wiser to fall back on an acknowledgement of our human limitations, and sing – if we must sing:

> We do not know, we cannot tell
> What pains He had to bear,
> But we believe it was for us
> He hung and suffered there.

Considering some of these, and other earlier theories, Dr Leslie Weatherhead, in our day, says, 'We must seek another interpretation of the Cross. For centuries men will wonder and adore, *but as far as understanding goes*, they will be Christian agnostics, and sing:

> We may not know, we cannot tell
> What pains He had to bear,
> But we believe it was for us
> He hung and suffered there.'

We are all different, and each comes to this great issue in the way that is most meaningful. For myself, this is now the New Testament word-picture of reconciliation. I look upon Christ's life and death – full of Love; and I see that when He faced the critical choice of *being put to silence about this*, or *being put to Death*, He had no doubt what His choice must be. His whole being – body, mind and spirit – was utterly committed to love, God's love, and His own. To the very last, as Paul contended: 'God was in Christ, *reconciling* the word unto Himself . . .' and (getting himself, and his fellow-Christians, into the picture in this great adventure in new values), added : 'and hath committed unto us *the word of reconciliation*.' (2 Corinthians 5 : 19). This is our Gospel to share. God the Father is, above all, love – sending this great reality to earth, through Jesus, expressed superbly in the Cross, and its final words of forgiveness – even for those who contrived that dastardly deed : 'Father, forgive them, for they know not what they do.' And there is no other power like that love. Here, committed to us – effective through faith – is our Gospel of reconciliation, between God and men, between us each and others.

But having said this much, words still have their limitations. I can only cast myself into this glorious mystery of love. I find myself borrowing Bishop F. R. Barry's summing up, in *Questioning Faith* : 'I do not think we can hope to understand what Christianity finds in the Cross, if we isolate the death of Christ either from the life of which it was the climax, or from the Resurrection and Pentecost, and continuing work of the living Christ in the Church, and through the Church in the wide world.' He finishes, 'That mistake has been one of the reasons which, in the past, have led so many theories into a cul-de-sac.'

So God's Love, in Christ, becomes saving Love !

So a timeless reality, becomes a personal reality.

In the issue of *The Expository Times*, which 'postie' has just brought me, the Reverend Owen Evans, of University College of North Wales, puts it plainly : 'If there is one word in the vocabulary of Christianity that ought to strike a sympathetic chord in the hearts of our contemporaries, it is surely the word *reconciliation*. The breakdown of personal relationships is an experience that was never commoner than it is today. So when the effect of Christ's saving work is described in terms of the mending of a broken personal relationship, it should mean more to the present generation than when other New Testament metaphors, drawn from such spheres as the slave market or the law courts, are employed . . . Nevertheless, no doctrine is adequate that does not see in the Cross the extent to which God's love is willing to go to reconcile man to Himself. In the New Testament, God is always the subject of reconciliation and man the object. It is the love of God that initiates the process of *reconciliation*.'

Sharing a meal shortly before his early death, my friend, Dr D. T. Niles from Ceylon, drew my attention to an incident recounted in his *Preaching the Gospel of the Resurrection*, and gave me in his own handwriting permission to pass on the Bishop's story given him. So it came to him – and to me – like this : 'Three university students of Paris were walking along the road on Good Friday afternoon. They noticed crowds of people going to the churches to make their confessions. The students began to discuss this custom of the "unenlightened", and talked together in rather cynical terms about the survival of religion, which they described as superstition. Suddenly two of the students said to the third, who was the leader among them, "Will you go into this church and tell the priest there what we have been saying to each other?" "Sure I will," he said, and went in. He stood in the queue of those who were going to confession and when his turn came, he looked at the priest and said, "Father, I have come to tell you that Christianity is a dying institution, and that religion is a superstition." The priest looked at the young man keenly, and said to him, "Why did you come here, my son, to tell me this?" And the student told him of his conversation with his friends. The priest listened carefully and said, "All right. I want you to do one thing for me before you go. You accepted the challenge of your friends and came here, now accept my challenge to you. Walk up to the chancel and you will find there a large wooden cross, and on it the figure of Jesus crucified. I want you to stand and say these words : 'Jesus died for me, and I don't care a damn.'" The student looked diffident, but to save face, agreed. He went up to the cross, and said, "Jesus died for me, and I don't care a damn." He came back to the priest and said, "I've done it." "Do it once more," said the priest, "it means nothing to you." The student went back, and looked at the cross for some time, and at the figure on it. Then he stammered out, "Jesus died for me, and I don't care." He returned to the priest and said, "I've done it; I'm going now." The priest stopped him. "Once more", he said, "just once more, and you can go." The young man walked up to the chancel and looked at that cross again, and at the crucified. He stood there for a long time, and then he said, *"Christ died for me."* Then he came back to the priest and said, "Father, can I make my confession now?"' The Bishop concluded the story with these unforgettable words: "And my dear people, that young man was myself".'

9. WHAT CHANGED THAT INSTRUMENT OF SHAME?

The most dastardly method of death did its worst on Calvary – the Son of Man, Son of God died on a Cross. Roman soldiers were hardened to the sight, as were most of the populace gathered there. Only a few of His friends could bear to stay to the end – a few of them 'afar off'.

'When the centurion, and they that were with him, watching Jesus saw . . . those things that were done, they feared greatly, saying, *"Truly, this was the Son of God!"*

'And many women were there beholding afar off, which followed Jesus from Galilee, ministering unto Him :

'When the even was come, there came a rich man of Arimathea named Joseph, who also himself was Jesus's disciple. He went to Pilate, and begged the body of Jesus . . . And when Joseph had taken the body, he wrapped it in a clean linen cloth, and laid it in his own tomb, which he had hewn out in the rock; and he rolled a great stone to the door of the sepulchre and departed.'

The disciples, stricken with grief, then locked themselves in 'for fear of the Jews'. And time hung heavy with them – especially, I suspect, the women, obliged to wait with idle hands. Little did any of them dream what lay ahead for them. They had left their occupations to follow Jesus – full of hope. And now the bottom had fallen out of their world. He had talked of a Kingdom – and though they had been slow to understand the full content of those words, they had not expected their relationship with Him to end like this. Only a few days ago, He had ridden into the Holy City like a King of Peace, with welcome from the crowds pulling down palm-branches, and scattering their cloaks in the way. All joined in the full-lunged welcome, 'Hosanna!' in the riotous manner of their times. Little did His jubilant disciples pause to calculate the possibility of a change of mood. And now it had come. Their eyes had looked on unbelievable happenings in that city where He had taught, and prayed, and ministered to its sick and distressed. From the Garden of Gethsemane the authorities had dragged Him forth; far into the night, He had stood trial – one after another taking part in the falsity of it all, its trumped-up charges, and its witnesses wearing the hours away. Then there had been a stripping, and a Cross to carry, fierce, harsh throats crying, 'Crucify Him! Crucify Him!' And trembling time favoured their whim; and crowds, some of them hardly knowing what it was all about, followed in the narrow streets. Simon-the-Negro, up from the country for the Passover maybe, found himself laid hold of by Roman soldiers, to bear that Cross love's full length. It was the last thing he had thought of doing when he set off from Cyrene – but he knew the law about carrying burdens, and he did not resist.

But during that grief-stricken wait behind doors, what could the women do? They made plans; and before the dawn of the third day sent its shafts of light into the Garden, with the tomb where they had tenderly left their Lord's body, Mary and her companions were on their way with spices for the embalming. And Life met her – instead of Death – her name spoken, catching her breath! And in a moment her feet took wings, and she was running with the news!

In that triumph, that cruel instrument of death, the Cross, became the symbol of redeeming love – of Christ alive for ever more!

And it remains that! When – between my two visits – the people of Coventry rebuilt their bombed cathedral, they employed a helicopter to set a great cross on its top-most pinnacle; and it was worth going back again to the city, to gaze upon it!

Dr J. S. Whale was speaking as a reverent theologian, when he said : 'The Gospels cannot explain the Resurrection : it is the Resurrection which alone explains the Gospels.' And much else – not least, the mighty transformation of Mary-of-the-Easter-Morning, and all those to whom the glorious news was brought. So tremendous was that experience that Thomas – one of that close company – refused to believe it on the witness of friends, till he had other proof.

In a short time – barred doors flung open, no longer counting fear a state to be dealt with – those men and women who had followed Jesus into the city, were about telling their story of an empty tomb, and One risen triumphant!

In a short time, as memories go, Paul was writing to his friends in Corinth: *'If Christ be not risen, then is our preaching vain, and your faith is also vain.'* (I Corinthians 15:14). He sees it all turning on that word 'If', and to make doubly clear, repeats it. *'If* Christ be not raised, your faith is vain; ye are yet in your sins. They also which are fallen asleep in Christ are perished. *If* in this life only we have hope in Christ, we are of all men most miserable.' (I Corinthians 15:17-19). These great issues do not turn on supposition, but on a certainty: a happening in history.

Halfway through the sixth volume of his *Study of History*, Professor Arnold J. Toynbee takes space to present the claims of those who, up through the centuries, have been counted 'saviours of society' – by the arts of war, powers of indoctrination, spoken words of wisdom. 'When we first set out on this quest', he says, 'we found ourselves moving in the midst of a mighty marching host; but as we have pressed forward on our way, the marchers, company by company, have been falling out of the race . . . In the last stage of all, our motley host of would-be saviours, human and divine, has dwindled to a single company of none but gods; and now the strain has been testing the staying-power of these last remaining runners, notwithstanding their superhuman strength. At the final ordeal of death, few, even of these would-be saviour-gods, have dared to put their title to the test by plunging into the icy river. And now as we stand and gaze with our eyes fixed upon the farther shore, *a single figure rises from the flood, and straightway fills the whole horizon. There is the Saviour: "and the pleasure of the Lord shall prosper in His hand; He shall see of the travail of His soul and shall be satisfied".'*

A single figure rises!

Many have done what they can to *refute* the Resurrection story – but their best has come to nothing. Frank

Morrison, in our day, was one such. Bringing his legal mind to bear on the evidence, he thought deeply; but ended up by completely altering his stance, and giving us his striking book : *Who Moved the Stone?* I am only one of thousands grateful to him. Not all have the trained mind to enable them to write so compellingly; they have to be content *to live in this world, lives of witness.* They acknowledge themselves Christians in every sense – claiming the truth of the Risen Christ, and His power to live in this complex modern world.

The record of the Resurrection is presented in considerable detail in all four Gospels. There is also, following on, the impressive list of witnesses' names given by Paul – with many of them still living when he wrote (I Corinthians 15 : 5-8). Apart from the renewal of the courage and character of the first disciple, the first day of the week – Christ's Resurrection Day – *replaced* the ancient seventh day for worship. Added to these striking points of persuasion, His world Church came into being.

The first of the opposing theories against the Resurrection claimed that *Jesus did not really die on the Cross, but merely swooned.* And when He was taken down for dead, and laid in the coolness of the tomb, He revived. After a while, these contend, He made His way out, and appeared to His disciples, and persuaded them that He had risen. But there are awkward points about this claim. To start with, Pilate had expressly provided against any such possibility, by ordering that the side of Jesus should be pierced. If the theory were true, the Crucified would have been also a wounded man; how He could have pushed open the entrance stone from the tomb, and escaped the Roman guards, must pose a problem. And how could He have persuaded the disciples, who knew Him so well, that He had overcome death? For weeks, if not longer, He must have been an invalid needing skilled care and rest. Added to these questions one must ask : 'If Jesus did not die on the Cross, where did He die?' The theory limps.

A second explanation offered is that the belief, which became widespread, that He had risen, owed its origin to *an hallucination suffered by Mary*, the first to meet

Him alive. This theory claims that, after all, she was a woman – over-wrought by the events shared, and lacking sleep. She imagined Him risen, and because she wished as much, suffered hallucination. But this theory is as unsatisfactory as the other. To begin with, hallucinations are not likely to occur, save when an event is eagerly expected and longed for. And nothing was further from the minds of the disciples – including Mary, and the rest of the women, sadly distraught at the time of the Crucifixion. Actually, one of the company, Thomas, even refused to believe it later, on the witness of his closest friends. More than this, the theory supposes that somehow the hallucinations became contagious, and spread for weeks, till several hundred people about were convincingly affected. But there is no record, in medical or psychiatric history, of hallucinations doing this. Moreover, it does not explain why the hallucinations ever ceased; nor how the tomb came to be empty.

Then there were some who contended that *it all hinged on a vision of Jesus in Heaven*, assuring them that all was well with Him. This might have accounted, in measure, for the revived spirit of His disciples – but it still leaves us to find some explanation for the empty tomb. It discredits the Gospel records, and without any real gain.

None of these theories adds up to anything, because they cannot face the simple fact that nobody seriously doubted the claims of the Christians at the time. They were men and women re-made, who began, with courage, to preach the Resurrection immediately – not long after, when some legend might have sprung up; and not in some distant place where little or nothing was heard of it – but where it had happened, and to those who had most to do with it.

The Resurrection – completely changing the Cross, that instrument of shame, to be, world round, a symbol of glory – is not a matter of legal argument; it is above all a matter of experience. *'The Resurrection of Christ is the only event of history'*, said Archbishop Anthony Bloom, over the BBC, *'that belongs both to the past and to the present.'* Changed lives – moving out from those first convinced disciples, to embrace countless millions of us men and women — is the undeniable answer.

Easter by Easter, I find myself declaring a reality that gives meaning to my life, lightness to my steps, and wonder to my words. My little poem : 'Easter Banners', broadcast lately, is simple enough; but it embraces an ageless reality :

> Hang out your hallelujahs !
> the Tomb is open,
> the Roman guard gone,
> Death defeated !
> The Man of Life walks again,
> comforting the troubled,
> healing the sick,
> forgiving sinners,
> spreading His Gospel through the lips
> and lives of men made new !

R.F.S.

10.   WHO IS THE HOLY SPIRIT?

It is not easy to put some deep realities into earth-words. 'Like all the deepest things in life', says Dr Ralph Sockman, distinguished Methodist radio man, 'the Holy Spirit is better apprehended *in action* than in definition.' So is the wind. And the two are often linked.

'The top of the hill is my favourite place', said a young companion to me lately, as we started to climb, 'because the air in a hurry there is so fresh. I like it.'

'Air-in-a-hurry' seemed a good name for the exhilaration we shared. That's the secret of the wind – it drives away stuffiness, smugness, lifelessness. No one of us can really live without an experience of the wind.

I think Jesus loved the wind. I think He raced as a youth upon those Nazareth hills, the wind in His hair. He remembered it once when He talked with Nicodemus, a ruler of the Jews, under the stars. He omitted nothing of loveliness, and what He caressed by look or word or hand became immortal. As He talked that night, I think, the wind blew where they sat and lightly touched His face and garments. A different place the world would be, had God not created the wind. There is such life in it; imagine a world where eternal calm held sway – an ocean with never a ripple, trees that never rocked, sultry days lacking exhilaration. But 'He bringeth the wind out of His treasuries'; and so in the skies of Jesus, winds blew, and poetry was in the night and on the land. And still it tugs at one's heart.

When God brought His Church into the world, *it was born in a wind*. There, at Pentecost, many knew it. The second chapter of the book of Acts attempts to set it down in words – though words are so limited. 'When the day of Pentecost was fully come', the record would have us know, 'they were all with one accord in one place. And suddenly there came a sound from heaven as of a *mighty rushing wind.*' That was His gift – exhilaration, liveliness, gladness. (Acts 2 : 1-2).

It was said of one of the early Christians that 'there was about him a breeze of freshness and hopefulness'. Surely, it should be characteristic of us Christians of every age; something is amiss if our religion results in stuffiness, in lifelessness. Being a Christian isn't just joining a congregation – it's an experience of life. And that's something more than morality touched with emotion. As soon as one speaks of the Spirit – known at Pentecost, but not by any means only there – that is what some people think. They only recognize this gift of God in certain ecstatic utterances, with a state of excitement that issues in hand-waving and clapping. The distinguished Scottish preacher and author, Dr James Stewart, in his recent book, *The Wind of the Spirit*, says : 'Always there are unmistakable signs when the power of the Spirit goes to work . . . When a man once weak and shifty and unreliable becomes strong and clean and victorious; when a church once stagnant and conventional and introverted throws off its dull tedium and catches fire and becomes alert and missionary-minded; when Christians of different denominations begin to realize there is far more in the Risen Christ to unite them than there can be anywhere else in the world or in their tradition to divide them; when religion, too long taboo in polite conversation, becomes a talking-point again; when decisions for Christ are seen worked out in family and business relationships; when mystic vision bears fruit in social passion – then indeed, the world is made to know that something is happening.'

'Speaking with tongues' is, as I see it, not alone proof of the presence of the Spirit; but witness in one's day-to-day life, of a Christ-like liveliness, is. The place where newness begins is in one's surrendered personality – reaching out in love, joy, peace, long-suffering, gentleness, goodness, faith, meekness, temperance – which Paul lists as 'the fruits of the Spirit' (Galatians 5 : 22). These lovely qualities add up to a kind of newness of which this tired old world stands badly in need. 'How little people know', says C. S. Lewis, 'who think that holiness is dull. When one meets

the real thing . . . it is irresistible.' It is not a negative
thing – any more than is the wind – it's a glorious, positive
reality, an exhilaration! And now! It is not limited to
Sundays, or hill-top experiences, or conferences. Exhilaration becomes never far-removed from each day's routine
– shopping, deciding what to cook, what to wear, how to
answer somebody's puzzling letter. It reaches out to all
life's daily concerns – it challenges the great national
issues. It fosters a lively courage; it may lead one into a
new job, into marriage, into politics, into authorship, into
service overseas. So one needs the consent of all one's
faculties to say:

> I see Thy light, *I feel Thy wind,*
> The world it is Thy word,
> Whatever wakes my heart and mind,
> Thy presence is, O Lord!

When Dr F. A. Cockin was writing his widely welcomed
book, *The Holy Spirit and the Church*, a friend suggested
to him, when it was in manuscript, that he had undertaken
an impossible task, and that it was unfair to ask anyone
to write a *real* book about the Spirit. Taxing it might be,
but surely not impossible. 'We may never know precisely
what happened at Pentecost', says Dr William Barclay,
'but we do know that it was one of the supremely great
days of the Christian Church, for on that day the Holy
Spirit came to the Christian Church in a very special
way.'

Today, many celebrate it with 'spirited' singing and
hand-clapping; and I do not deny that a quickened
religious reality has come to many through this. But it
cannot be the only way. 'Tarry ye in the city of Jerusalem',
the first Christians were instructed. In the new power that
was given them, they were soon involved in out-going
experiences. The Spirit, we are told, moved Philip to
establish a surprising relationship with an Ethiopian
eunuch (Acts 8:29); and prepared Peter for entry into

a new experience of outreach, when the messengers of Cornelius arrived (Acts 11:12); ordered the setting apart of Paul and Barnabas for the important step of taking the Gospel to the hitherto overlooked Gentiles (Acts 13:2-4); guided the decisions of the Church Council in Jerusalem (Acts 15:28); led Paul, in his preliminary plans to journey in Asia, down by way of Troas into Europe – changing the whole world-pattern of history, and our lives now.

But the action of the Spirit did not, of course – though many forget it – start with the mighty rushing wind and exhilaration of Pentecost. God's Spirit was present, brooding over shapeless elements in creation, at the very first; providing later the well-spring of inspiration for the prophets; guiding those responsible for the governing of the chosen nation before God's face; taking hold of an individual here and there, for special service. At the beginning of the New Testament era, Scripture says Jesus was conceived by the Holy Spirit – to Mary, the village maiden, was given the promise, 'The Highest shall overshadow thee' (Luke 1:35). A like promise came concerning His fore-runner, John the Baptist (Luke 1:67). Then, when Jesus stepped down into the waters of Jordan, ready for His life-work, 'the Holy Ghost descended in bodily shape like a dove upon Him, and a voice came from heaven, which said, "Thou art My beloved Son; in Thee I am well pleased".' (Luke 3:22). His ministry throughout was performed in the power of the Spirit – His speaking and healing, His acts of forgiveness and reconciliation. After His death, Rising-again, and Ascension, His followers were encouraged to count on a new awareness of the Spirit. 'When the Comforter is come, whom I will send unto you from the Father,' said Jesus, whilst still with them in bodily form, 'even the Spirit of truth, which proceedeth from the Father, he shall testify of Me; and ye shall bear witness.' (John 15:26-27).

But I do not here, or anywhere in the New Testament, read that there is to be only one way of His reception, only one way of witness to that reality. Ecstatic utterance – call it what you will, 'speaking with tongues' is not the only proof of His presence. Even in the early days, Paul expressed himself as a little uneasy about it (I Corinthians 14 : 18-19). 'I thank my God, I speak with tongues more than ye all,' said he, 'yet in the church I had rather speak five words with my understanding, that by my voice I might teach others also, than ten thousand words by an unknown tongue.'

Paul is not here condemning 'tongues' outright – but he puts them down below the power of prophecy, and away down below *the possession of love*, and the daily expression of it. 'If I speak with the tongues of men and of angels', he says in another letter (I Corinthians 13 : 1) *'and have not love*, I am become sounding brass or a clanging cymbal' – something merely noisy.

Paul even dared to say : 'Tongues . . . shall cease' (v.8). Chrysostom declared that the gift became non-existent in the fourth century. In more recent times – and notably in many parts in our day – men and women of religious fervour have again broken out into incomprehensible utterance. Their voices raised have even, at times, put the preacher to silence. Monsignor Ronald Knox, in his famous study, *Enthusiasm*, tells of a Mary Campbell, who announced that she had 'the gift of tongues'. To those nonplussed by the spate of incoherent sounds that she uttered, she claimed to be speaking in Turkish, and in the language of the Pelew Islands – languages she had never learned. She even thought of going as a missionary to convert the heathen in those places.

In the same widely-accepted study, Knox lists words as typical of 'tongues' uttered in the congregation of the fashionable Presbyterian preacher of the last century, Edward Irving – 'words beyond the reach of the lexicon : *hippo gerosto niparos boorastin farini O fastor sungar boorinos spoongos menanti.'*

I am satisfied that I must pay attention to Paul's warning – words are not enough, though spoken with the eloquence 'of men and of angels'. There is another test, and a final – close to our everyday witness – the possession of what Paul calls 'the fruits of the Spirit' (Galatians 5 : 22-

23). These Christ-like gifts are recognizable anywhere. 'Against these', Paul sums up, 'there is no law'. (Some, of course, who lay great emphasis on 'speaking with tongues', know this too.)

So I try to be fair; and set against my own experience of the Spirit those lovely qualities listed by Paul. This always humbles me. But it helps to make more meaningful my recital of the Apostles' Creed, as a member of our congregation : *'I believe in the Holy Spirit'*. And there have been times when I have shared in a service where the Nicene Creed has been intoned majestically : *'I believe in the Holy Ghost . . .'* A modern affirmation – with which I could join – declares : *'We believe in the Holy Spirit as the divine presence in our lives, whereby we are kept in perpetual remembrance of the truth of Christ, and find strength and help in time of need.'*

A reality everyday – Whit Sunday may prove a day above others when one's responsiveness is most clear. Lately, I titled a poem *Whit Sunday* :

> Today, I would celebrate God's kindled flame –
> with colours blended;
> *His wind* – with feelings given power;
> I would adventure forth
> into earth's ways,
> with valiant courage, and gentleness,
> supporting every living soul with respect,
> sending no child loveless to bed.
> I would fill my wallet with songs
> that set failures
> on their feet in hard places;
> I would fill my wallet with songs
> across the sordid and the dull,
> strengthening wills with purpose
> and clear joy,
> sharing the one Gospel.
> Love holds its dynamic – faith and hope
> supporting company,
> as speech and silence, precious
> as action and ease,

values of the Young King,
    triumphant as the raptures of lovers,
or one's own language spoken suddenly
    in a strange land !

R.F.S.

11. WHAT IS THE CLOSEST NAME FOR GOD?

Jesus talked about the Fatherhood of God. What did He mean by that? He was not the first to use the term — it occurred in the Old Testament with which He had been familiar from His childhood up. Jesus was a Jew, and, like His contemporaries, took the existence of God for granted. Monotheism, the belief that there is but one God, was early and deeply ingrained in the national character. The term 'Father' was used to describe God's relationship with the nation, and occasionally with the individual. Rabbinical prayers used the term in Jesus's time. (In Babylonia, in Egypt, in Greece and in Rome, that gracious name was already in use. In the third century before Jesus used it, the great stoic philosopher Cleanthes prayed : 'Draw men out from the gloom of their ignorance, scatter the darkness of their souls, O Father.')

But when Jesus took the name on His lips, *He imbued it with a new content*. He took the name 'Father' that hovered about the circumference of men's thought, and put it at the centre. The Gospels show how all through His life, from boyhood up till He hung upon His Cross between earth and heaven, this term of address most closely expressed what He felt about God. His earliest recorded saying is not easily forgotten : 'Wist ye not that I must be about *My Father's business*?' And His last expiring utterance as a man is even more impressive : *'Father*, into Thy hands I commend My spirit !'

Very little is recorded of His early family life. We wish we knew more, especially of Joseph. But as one scholar has said : 'In the first sentence of the Lord's Prayer, he has a monument which reaches up to heaven. What he is saying, is : If Joseph had not been a wonderful man, in his relationships, Jesus could never have used that term "Father", for God. "If ye then, being evil, know how to give good gifts unto your children", said Jesus, "*how much more* shall your Father give good gifts to them that ask Him?" '

One of the most winsome religious poems I know is one that a poet of our day, Gilbert Thomas, has given us, to express this confidence :

Who has not carolled Mary,
And who her praise would dim?
But what of humble Joseph?
Is there no song for him?

If Joseph had not driven
Straight nails through honest wood,
If Joseph had not cherished
His Mary as he should,

If Joseph had not proved him
A sire both kind and wise,
Would he have drawn with favour
The Child's all-probing eyes?

Would Christ have prayed '*Our Father*',
Or cried that name in death,
Unless He first had honoured
Joseph of Nazareth?

Martin Luther had to confess that because of what his father was, he could not use the term 'father' without a shudder; and there are others known to me today who must confess as much. Some, indeed, do not even know who their fathers are. But as Jesus used the term, it meant much. 'Jesus's proclamation of the Divine Fatherhood', as Dr George Duncan says, in *Son of Man*, 'is something very different from the enunciation of a general truth that God is the Father of all men, and that all men are His sons. By His preaching and teaching, by His words of mercy and power, by the whole character of His life, Jesus gave to the world a new demonstration of the Divine Fatherhood in action.'

So, when His disciples begged Our Lord to teach them

to pray, He began with that great and hallowed name,
Our Father – and men and women of faith have been
using it ever since, till now not an hour passes but it rises
somewhere. It is taught to us as children, it serves to
express mature attitudes of the heart when the sun is high,
it speaks the comfort and assurance needed by old folk
when the shadows fall – it is spoken in private, and has its
place within all services of the Church. Beginning with
that lovely name, clause by clause, it is close to life. Our
habit of running through it at breakneck speed, or using
it thoughtlessly, is always a loss. Familiarity can do desperate things to any rich possession. Dr Edwin Muir, college
warden, poet, traveller, tells us in his autobiography what
it came to mean for him, in a moment of quiet sincerity
and illumination. Said he : 'Last night, going to bed alone,
I suddenly found myself (I was taking off my waistcoat)
reciting the "Lord's Prayer" in a loud, emphatic voice – a
thing I had not done for many years – with deep urgency
and profound, disturbed emotion. While I went on I grew
more composed . . . every word had a strange fitness of
meaning which astonished and delighted me. It was late;
I had sat up reading; I was sleepy; but as I stood in the
middle of the floor half-undressed, saying the prayer over
and over, meaning after meaning sprang from it, over-
coming me again with joyous surprise !'

From the moment I first gave attention to that prayer;
first read of Jesus's answer to Philip's question in the
Upper Room : 'He who hath seen Me, hath seen the
Father . . .'. and read of His last use of the beloved name
as He closed His eyes on the Cross, it has become as
meaningful to me as to Edwin Muir.

When Jesus first introduced to His disciples – and in turn,
to us – that pattern prayer, His introductory words were
'When you pray . . .' not *'If* you pray . . .' for He knew
we wouldn't get far without calling upon God. For to
pray is as natural to men and women as to breathe, to eat,
to sleep. Carelessness might seem to contradict this in the
lives of many of us; but any crisis, any sudden sense of
insufficiency, will stir us to prayer, as naturally as to reach
out for support when falling. We have only to stand beside

a hospital bed when some modern drug has failed; to receive sudden news of an accident; to be involved in a breach of family faith; or at the other extreme, joyously to welcome a little new life into the home; to have some important professional purpose succeed; to be sustained in a testing moment through the warm understanding of others, and we pray.

Of course, this great prayer, to *God our Father* – twenty centuries after it was first given – needs to be prayed intelligently, and with the consent of all our faculties. Dr George Morrison – loved minister of Wellington Church, Glasgow, where I was once honoured to stand where he had long stood, to speak to a packed church of women-folk – made this discovery. His mind was often so crowded with concerns when he paused for private prayer, that there came a moment when he determined *not* to get up from his knees, until he had prayed – not just repeated the Lord's Prayer through, with its wonderful beginning, leading on to each of its clauses. Again and again, he began, *and ten times failed*, only to succeed at the eleventh time. But it made a world of difference ever afterwards. (I was moved to have Bishop Robinson – author of *Honest to God*, the most discussed religious book in our sophisticated generation – say, 'I do not pray to "The Ground of my Being", I pray to *God the Father* . . . to the utterly gracious personal Reality which Jesus could only address as "Abba, Father". I have no interest in a God conceived in vaguely impersonal terms.'

The time came for me, in my search for practical religion, when I realized that to pray *'Our Father which art in heaven'*, implied *'our brother who is on earth'*. History is littered with experiments in 'brotherhood-living' which have come to naught – and we have them in our society today – because their promoters have not seen these two realities tied together. Our challenge is to learn how to work out their relationships in all its ramifications. And not only in our human family is this essential, but in our community life with its colliding interests, and in the wide world of hunger, selfish political aims, and inter-national notions that lead to war, the proliferation of nuclear missiles, and annihilation.

This involves us all – as witnessing Christians, voters in local and in national elections, readers, travellers amidst international affairs, with race prejudices, and widespread, practical claims for good. Not only does it concern the masses, but respect for every individual, since we are all in one sense, if not by active faith, God's children. Jesus placed such emphasis on the value of one, in His lovely parables of the lost son; the lost coin hunted for high and low; and the lost sheep, searched for at great cost of effort by the shepherd who had already ninety-and-nine safe at home.

To make this essential yet more clear, Jesus spoke of sparrows. (In Jerusalem, I have myself seen them in the crevices of the city walls. In the little-used streets, their cheerful, concerted chat threatens every other sound.) Any member of a modest family, who did the buying, with small coins, would make his or her way into the market, in Jesus's time, to find offered there piles of the little creatures, plucked and trussed on wooden skewers. And He remembered always those transactions, when as a lad, He had 'done the messages'. He spoke of '*two* sparrows sold for a farthing' (Matthew 10:29). And again, of '*Five* sparrows sold for two farthings' (Luke 12:6). He was not momentarily confused – He was saying that sparrows were of such small value individually, that when a householder could afford the larger purchase, a little extra bird was thrown in for nothing, a good bargain. 'Yet', said He, 'one of them shall not fall on the ground *without your Father* . . .' And moving to His favourite 'how much more' argument, He added: 'Fear ye not, ye are of *more value* than many sparrows'.

Today, we move in a large society, where the individual is easily lost, submerged in a terrible meaninglessness, valuelessness. Once deeply believe that God is our Father, and this cannot be – we have this on the authority of Jesus. It is a reality that makes all the difference to life. In Harnack's words: 'Jesus Christ was the first to bring *the value of every human soul to light*, and what He did, no one can ever more undo.'

So we, one by one, use the word 'Father' when praying or thinking about God, with Whom we seek a close relationship, not because we feel it an adequate term of address, but because it is the least inadequate we know. And the sheer wonder of it brings joy and sudden radiance. For the peace and undertone of meaning is that everything we experience comes to us within the knowledge of God. 'We see Him at last', as Dr Rufus Jones, the Quaker leader says, 'we know now what He is like, we are confined no longer to abstract attributes, such as "infinite", "omniscient" and "absolute". We come closer into the heart of things, and find that the highest and most exalted Being is *our Father, Who had all along been seeking us while we were feeling our way to Him.*'

12. ISN'T PRAYER VERY DIFFICULT?

Well, yes, sometimes it is – when I'm not in the mood for it; when I've let it lapse for even a day, for any reason at all; when I'm preoccupied with many interests. Prayer is not something that can be done in a scrambling hurry – any more than is friendship, family love, great music, and fine books and art. It is not an obligation – it's a privilege.

And it has two parts – to miss either is a loss almost as desperate as to miss both. The Psalmist sets them together in his experience, as I learned to do when I entered into the true meaning of prayer. His words are: *'Hear me* speedily, O Lord . . .' (Psalm 143 : 7), and in the very next breath: *'Cause me to hear . . .* !' (v. 8).

Even though one might not start with 'Our Father', the words Jesus taught with all the wonderful, far-reaching implications that form of address carries, I must be aware of God's presence. As Dr Harry Fosdick introduces this vital experience: 'Prayer is not crying to a mysterious individual off somewhere; prayer is not bouncing the ball of one's own aspiration against the wall of one's own soul, and catching it again; true prayer is fulfilling one of the major laws of the spiritual world and getting appropriate consequences.' It is a close relationship with God – one's need, one's ignorance, one's frustration, human frailty, ecstasy, thankfulness, all part of it. So that it is never static – though I use the same prayer-book again and again, to set me going; or pray directly in my own staggering sentences. Nor is it a small, or casual undertaking. 'When we pray', says Alexis Carrell, scientist of wisdom, 'we link ourselves with the inexhaustible motive power that spins the universe.'

And it can happen at any time, in any place. I have not to go to the ends of the earth to begin, to learn by heart great and impressive words; or wait till I am a worthier character before I pray. I can pray, using the words that serve me, here and now. A new day comes – and feeling inadequate, I pray; someone dear to me falls sick – and I pray; one in whom I have placed my confidence lets me down – and I pray; a big task confronts me, and possessing all too little experience and human strength, I pray.

The pity is that for so many of us is it only a *crisis* experience. If we could pray but once a week, once a year, or once in twenty-five years, how greatly we would value it. When I spent a day walking around St Peter's in Rome, Austin Phelps's word-picture came back to me, with even more striking significance than when I learned of it first. 'In the vestibule of St Peter's is a doorway, which is walled-up and marked with a cross. It is opened but four times in a century . . . Then the Pope approaches it in princely state, with the retinue of cardinals in attendance, and begins the demolition of the door, by striking it three times with a silver hammer. When the passage is opened, the multitude pass into the nave of the cathedral, and up to the altar, by an avenue the majority of them never entered before, and never will enter thus again.' I paid special attention to this when I visited St Peter's; and since then on TV, watching one midday at a friend's home – I saw the whole impressive ceremony, almost as if I was myself present. And I shall never forget it.

'Imagine', says Austin Phelps, 'that the way to the Throne of Grace were like the Porta Sancta, inaccessible, save once in a quarter of a century. Conceive that it were now ten years since you, or I, or any other sinnner, had been permitted to pray; and that twenty-five long years must drag themselves away, before we could venture again to approach God, and that, at the most, we could not hope to pray more than two or three times in a lifetime! With what solicitude we should wait for the coming of that Holy Day!' It might well be that you and I too easily miss one of life's great privileges, because it is so commonplace. Because we can pray at *any time*, some of us pray at no time – unless a crisis breaks in upon us. Then like Peter, who fell into the sea when he attempted to walk on it, we cry one by one: 'Lord, help me!' If this is our attitude, is it any wonder that for the greater part of life, prayer is a little unreal?

And it can be as unreal if we think of prayer only as a divinely-provided *shortcut for getting things*. There have been times when I have needed to be delivered from some impending disaster, as surely as did Peter – and I have been delivered. A garage-hand once let me out on to the hilly, winding approach to Dunedin, at the busiest traffic time, with faulty brake-bands he'd been asked to fix, un-fixed. It was a crisis situation, since the highway was so steep, and I had my heavily-laden van and caravan, twenty-four feet in total length, to manage alone. I got down!

But I do not expect to have to pray like that very often. Prayer is a natural, daily, on-going event; in the lovely words of the Catechism of the United Church of Canada: 'Prayer is laying our lives open before God in gratitude and expectancy, casting ourselves on His mercy and love, *telling* Him all the desires of our hearts, *listening* to His voice, and *accepting* His way for our lives.' In short, it is fellowship with God – communion, if you find that word more real. It is entering into a relationship that God, out of the deep wisdom and love of His heart, desires; it is not nudging His elbow to do for me what I want, it is my utter readiness and humble desire to do *what He wants.*

Communion with God, through prayer, means – as Father Mark Gibbard, with much experience in our day, says – 'marvelling at God's love, receiving it, responding to it, being united with it and sharing it in the world – so that we can live contemplatively and constructively . . Prayer goes dull unless our understanding of God, and our wonder at His love, are growing, just as our friendships lose their warmth and sometimes peter out, if we are not *growing* in understanding, appreciation and *openness to one another.*'

It is a good thing, I find, to spend some time in preparation for prayer – to find a place where I'm not likely to be interrupted. (This is a modern equivalent of the Master's injunction, 'Enter thy closet, and shut thy door.') Sometimes, if the weather is right, it is a good experience to pray out of doors, walking along a quiet road, or a beach. Sometimes, I find, it is easiest to pray standing, at other times, kneeling, at yet other times, lying on the sweet-smelling grass, or on my bed. The great thing is to have one's body at ease, so that its claims do not obtrude. Then one's mind, one's spirit have a better chance of being free. Pins-and-needles in the knees have more than once defeated my spirit of devotion. Sometimes, it is a help to read to oneself a passage of Scripture first; sometimes, to look up at a lovely colour picture of the hills, if they are too far removed in actuality to look at with their quiet, aspiring dignity. Others find a sea picture, or a picture of a great tree, uprising, outreaching, as great a help. For others again, a simple cross on a table or book-case ledge, can gather up all these meanings – and more – as the word-pictures of Jesus come refreshingly, challengingly from the Gospels. Speaking of 'Letting the mind run down', Monica Furlong – the journalist whom I quoted with delight early in this book – says: 'I don't think – amateurs at prayer, as most of us are – that we pay half enough attention to pre-prayer . . . If prayer is, as I believe, not a matter of uttering a few words, even if deeply felt, but of achieving a certain sort of creative *awareness*, then it is idle to suppose that this can be fitted in, like physical jerks, between dressing and eating breakfast.' And what does well for one of us will not serve another at all. Several known to me, who live in a crowded hostel, and one who stays in a home where there are small children, set off for work in the morning fifteen minutes early, and pop into a church on the way. From time to time, they manage half an hour – though time isn't the only thing, if one can get peace around, and within.

I find it helpful to take a few deep breaths; to keep a moment's silence; to go on to remember where I am, and why; and what my day's obligations are. I ask for courage to pray sincerely – and to listen – in the brief space I have. Sometimes, in that quietness, I have confessions to make, problems to mention, areas of doubt to admit, breaches of human relations to acknowledge.

I don't always get instant, and exact, answers – but often

something much better: *awareness of God*, and power to see my particular need from a new point of view.

In prayer it is so necessary to avoid religious clichés, to shun the temptation to draw a line between things 'sacred' and 'secular'; to tell God what I want Him to do: one must come in a humble, asking, seeking frame of mind, prepared to be perfectly honest, to tell Him that one can't have patience with So-and-So much longer; that one's faith is terribly feeble, and one is ashamed that it is so; that one is tempted to buy things for which one ought not to spare the money. What good can come of any undertaking where there is pious pretence?

Those lose much in this relationship who only want God's help when things are difficult, and they are bothered, or defeated. Some think it mean to call upon God only at such times, so they don't pray at all. And they feel pretty virtuous in their attitude. Another – a strong extrovert – will claim: 'I manage, all in all, by myself – I don't need to pray. It seems rather a form of weakness – a "bolt-hole".' If Christians from the start had taken this attitude – praying only when life came at them round an awkward corner – the wonder and worth of prayer would not have reached us in this generation.

And many another – friend, neighbour, awkward office clerk, young airman, shy hesitant soul, hot-tempered member of the family – would have missed much. For *intercession* is a very valuable part of this prayer experience. Paul discovered this, early on; and his letters to friends are sprinkled with references to this privilege. In a letter to friends at Colossae he writes: 'We have never ceased to pray for you, asking God to fill you with the knowledge of His Will . . .' (Colossians 1 : 9, Moffatt). Again, to others, the Thessalonians, he writes: 'In view of this [some situation between them] we always pray for you, asking our God to make you worthy of His calling.' (II Thessalonians 1 : 11; Moffatt).

This is neither to coerce God, nor to curry favour; it is to outreach to others in loving care, beyond one's own powers, out to the powers of a caring Father. He is Almighty. Therefore one need not prescribe *how* He shall act; nor, because He is all-wise, and loving, *when*.

Someone has fittingly called intercession, '*Love upon its knees*'. It often happens that this ministry in a comunity is exercised gladly and faithfully by a quiet soul, crippled sometimes, hindered from doing more active things; or it may be that age keeps a friend of prayer house-bound – whilst strength is poured into many busy lives. One whom I know well, in an effort to make his prayer relevant in this demanding world, takes the newspaper into his prayer-room, or another time takes his church paper, and reads them quietly, praying for each reported to be in grief; in the hands of the Law; in a position of grave decision-making. (One needs time, of course, to do this.)

Lately, I found myself fashioning a 'Storm Prayer':

> O God – what a night to be out!
> The wind sings falsetto all round,
> and strong trees thrash their boughs about.
> Rain has forgotten her kindness,
> to be a stubborn fury let loose,
> beating in anger and blindness.
> Have pity, Lord, on the new-born,
> and the aged, come to death's doorstep,
> and all creatures but newly shorn.
> Bless those boring through dark's despair,
> the ill, and all cheated of sleep,
> sea-captains, and those in the air.
> And bless especially this night
> all on mercy bent – here, and now :
> *Lead us, Lord, to the new day's light!*
>
> R.F.S.

There are, of course, what are called 'answers to prayer'. 'Answers to prayer?', asks Dr W. H. Fitchett, listing a number. 'Who shall classify them, remember them, or measure them? They are made up of deliverances, comforts, pardons, illuminations, strange endowments of strength to the weak, of courage to the fearful, and of guidance to the perplexed.' We each know at some time what it is to be perplexed. But how does God's guidance come?

Life brings me constantly to the crossroads of choice. It is only when I come to look back that I am sure of *the ways* guidance comes. And they are many. It is easy to sing with others William Williams's hymn, 'Guide me, O Thou great Jehovah', with its splendid tune, *Cym Rhondda*, and be a bit vague about it. He wrote it originally, away back; twenty-five years later it was translated into English by the Reverend Peter Williams of Carmarthen. But its author wasn't satisfied with his compatriot's effort; so he made another rendering – and that's the one we have today.

It marches to one's need, with a great and glorious confidence – and that is a good thing. But God's guidance is in no sense limited to church – it would be a sorry state of things, if it were – though life in the congregation is a likely place in which to discover it.

Nor is it a vague, comfortable, supporting relationship. Arthur Mee, a loved editor, said : 'We know there is Something not ourselves, that comes with us through the years, which gives us strength in weakness, courage in failure, endurance in long-suffering, and the assurance that, whatever may befall, our destiny is secure. *He guides us, and the bird,* along our pathless way, and in His good time, we shall arrive.'

But often, when perplexed, one wants to know what to do *now*, so that a pressing situation can be met, and lead on into the future. It is all part of life – one has to learn. This is God's world; and He guides us, beginning where we are.

When perplexed, it is not easy to know that there is a place for patience. If we have brought all our powers of thought and experience to the problem on hand, and cannot see our way ahead, it may be that we must regard this as present guidance. It may be that we have to endure the situation, and wait. Most choices have to be made from a mingling of right and wrong, of immediate and ultimate good. It isn't always simple. 'This does not mean that "waiting upon God" is useless', as the Very Reverend W. R. Matthews, Dean of St Paul's, was moved to remind us. 'Some people seem to suppose that if they say a prayer and then make their minds a blank, the first notion that occurs to them is guidance. This, I believe, is dangerous nonsense. We have to use our minds and think as hard as we can. Then, when we have worked at the problem, and perhaps are still uncertain what we ought to do, it is well to be quiet and still in the presence of God. When we are prepared and ready to hear, the word of God may come to us clearing up our perplexities.' Cosmo Gordon Lang found it so. (It seems strange, at first, that a young man, who later became Archbishop of Canterbury, could ever have hesitated.) He was deeply troubled at one stage as to whether or not his real place was in the priesthood. One weekend he was in Oxford, and on the Sunday afternoon accompanied a friend, on foot, to Cuddesdon. 'I went to the Parish Church', said he later, 'for evensong. The whole scene is indelibly impressed upon my memory. I sat in the second pew from the pulpit. I paid little attention to the service, and less to the sermon, which was preached by the curate. But I had a strong sense that something was about to happen. I was not in the least excited; there was no sort of nervous tension; I had only prayed in a rather weary way during the service in some such manner as this : "I can't go on with this strange struggle. End it, O God, one way or the other." Then, suddenly, while the unheeded sermon went on, I was gripped by a clear conviction. It had all the strength of a masterful inward voice.

"*You are wanted. You are called. You must obey.*" I knew at once the thing was settled. The burden of the long struggle dropped. My mind was free. I don't want to write emotionally, but it is only recording fact to say that a wave of such peace and indeed joy as I had never known before filled my whole being.'

Guidance needs careful testing with another, whose spirit of devotion one can trust – wishful thinking can so easily deceive one.

And, at the other extreme, one needs to be wise, and show some reserve, when listening to an eager friend or acquaintance who exclaims : 'God said to me . . .', or 'I was guided . . .', or any similar statement.

And, of course, it is a mistake to think that God's guidance can come only through a vision or some extra-ordinary experience. It may be, but not necessarily so. God can guide us – and often does – through very down-to-earth happenings. I think of Margaret Bonfield, to balance a man's experience with that of a woman, seeking a life-work. Born in Somerset, she became Assistant Secretary of the Shop Assistants' Union, rose to be Chairman of the TUC, entered Parliament and became the first woman to achieve Cabinet rank. But it all started very modestly. 'Being hungry one night', she said, looking back, 'I bought "a penn'orth of fish and a ha'p'orth of chips", that great standby of the very poor. It was wrapped in a bit of newspaper which I read while munching the food, sauntering around Fitzroy Square. It contained a letter from James Macpherson, Secretary of the National Union of Shop Assistants, Warehousemen and Clerks, urging all shopworkers to join up and fight for better conditions in their trade. My conversion was instantaneous and for three years my scanty leisure was given to my union. We had about six campaigns running – for more wages, against fines and deductions, against the living-in system, against secret references, against radius agreements, above all, for more leisure. Ah ! they were splendid days ! To me at that time, the denial of privacy was my greatest trial . . . My hours of work were from 7.30 a.m. to 8.30 or 9 p.m., with three breaks for breakfast, dinner and tea. Supper was served after the shop closed. My wage was £25 per annum, paid monthly. A rush at closing time to get to the union branch meeting usually meant a fish and chip supper out of the scanty wage; often, too, a rush to get back again before one got locked out at 10.30 p.m. – lights out at 11 p.m. We slept four in a room.'

A quiet service in a country church, or a piece of paper around a meal of fish and chips! God can use all manner of things to guide His helpers into their right sphere of service in His world. And he can guide you and me – indeed, has guided me again and again, in my responses. Looking back – to write an autobiography, or just to remember with thanks – nothing is more real.

Often – as must be now plain – *God guides us through circumstances.* Sometimes it may be a big matter, like finding one's life-work; at another time, finding how best to do some part of it, perhaps new and perplexing; or to extend some opportunity for special training; or to recognize some unfolding possibility.

Again, *God can guide one through people.* One may be induced to think of an interest entirely new, by the enthusiasm of a friend; or because one meets a person one admires; or because it is much talked of in the set in which one moves. Or it may be that He guides one, through suddenly becoming aware of the desperate state of certain people – at home, or overseas – and one is led to give one's money, or one's service. To be shown that 'People are people wherever you meet them', as Dame Edith Evans declares, is to be guided often into a new sense of responsibility towards them – black people, yellow people, brown, white, illiterate, hungry, lonely, ill-clad, affluent. It matters not that one must continue in one's job, club, church, community – one's life can never be the same again; one is more aware of God, because one is more aware of His people, and one's daily life takes on new shapes and colours, richer than ever before. I know it.

God can guide us through worship; through prayer; through Bible reading – if approached reverently, intelligently, expectantly. (You may even have counted on my putting these long-tested ways first. I don't know that that matters; one thing is certain – He expects us to seek guidance with the co-operation and consent of all our faculties.) In these days when there are so many ways of learning truth, ignorance, apathy, lovelessness are inexcusable. We are not children any more – we are dwellers in this twentieth-century world where men and women build homes, and places of business and learning, give birth to children, paint, dance and sing, sow seed and harvest, share skills, make war, and walk on the moon.

We are called to love God with all our heart, all our soul, and all our mind. For some, still, nothing is so uncomfortable as a new thought, nothing so awkward as a new alliance. The one essential, of course, is that we should seek to be guided. Naturally, we must not think of any one of these ways as excluding another – sometimes God combines several to guide us graciously.

The conditions of this add up to a fourfold acceptance. *We must utterly accept our Guide; we must be travelling His way; we must be continually open to receive guidance; we must be ready to act on the guidance given.*

There are hours, of course, when guidance seems clearer than at others. A man wrote to *The Times* to tell about his early Sunday morning task, which was to climb the spire of St Michael's Church, which crowns Highgate Hill in North London, to wind the clock. Sometimes, he confessed, as he looked out from that great height, he could see nothing – mist completely blotted out his view. But there were other times when the sun pierced the mist, and there at his feet lay all the glory of London. 'How like the religious life', he added. 'We go regularly to church and often nothing seems to happen. But then, one morning, the mists, as it were, fall apart, and the Son of Righteousness arises with healing in His wings!'

14. HOW MUCH DOES RELIGION ALLOW QUESTIONS?

There may be forms of religion where all matters have long been closed, where there is no room for questioning. But that is not our Christian faith.

The first word-picture we have of the youth Jesus shows Him, during His first visit to Jerusalem, in the Temple, 'in the midst of the doctors, both *hearing and asking them questions*'. Many artists, including Hofmann, have given us a quite wrong impression of this; they have shown the youth standing erect amidst the 'grey beards', as if authoritively expounding the truth to them. This was not at all how it was that day, when Mary and Joseph, supposing Him to have gone on with friends, in the home-going caravan found it wasn't so. After anxiously returning, they found Him, behaving in quite a natural way in the Temple – not standing, *seated*, as the Gospel says. He did not figure there with overbearing confidence – He was a natural questioner, so young, that there were many things He wanted to know. Question and answer was then the method by which the doctors of the Law taught.

And through all the centuries since, there has been a place in Christianity for the questions – no matter how young. Question-asking, like charity, it has been said, begins at home – and that is healthy enough. 'Every normal child', Dorothy Sayers rejoiced to say, 'is a walking interrogation-mark.' And she hadn't need to be a distinguished detective-writer to make that discovery – every parent, aunt, uncle, teacher, neighbour amongst us knows as much. And often the questions are religious questions. 'When does God sleep?' 'Is God really Almighty – can He do anything?' 'Is God interested in the Space-age?' 'What makes Him let suffering happen?' These are only a few that I have overheard – and they are all *religious questions*. Young boys and girls, in this modern age, still want to know things. And the questions are very pertinent. A little note-book that has turned up records the questions the Reverend

Jonathan Edwards was asked away back in 1730. Little John Baker then wanted to know: 'Which of the Kings of Israel and Judah reigned longest?' Can you imagine any little twentieth-century boy you know caring one way or the other? I can't. And the question which came from little Timothy Wright, in that same year, was: 'Which of the three sons of Noah did Egyptians come from?' I can't imagine any little present-day Timothy – who knows the top-speed of every jet plane, and every car – caring a jot about the Egyptians. The questions that crop up in Bible knowledge periods nowadays have a different feel about them. The familiar Christmas story – with Joseph and Mary locked out of the inn – brought forth the unselfconscious question: 'Why didn't Joseph *book*?'

If, growing up from childhood, through youth, we cannot ask our questions as Jesus did, in the house of God, *where indeed can we ask them* with the expectation of a helpful answer?

'Faith', of course, 'there must be', as Dr Ronald Wright, leader of St Giles's Club for youth in Edinburgh, says in the series of books proudly associated with his name, *Asking them Questions*, based on the experience of the youth Jesus in the Temple. 'Argument', says one of the contributors, 'generally speaking, in religion can do no more than clear the track; but there is no reason for not clearing the track. But the word "faith", if we are not careful, can often become just another word for laziness. Our Lord *studied the Scriptures*, and as we have seen, *asked questions.*'

'Some questions', one has said, 'can be meaningless'. Perhaps the question 'Who made God?' is one of them, like the question: 'Where did God stand when He made the world?'

But the interrogation-mark is not by any means confined to childhood and youth. The Bible, as we adults come to it, is sprinkled with 'Wheres?' and 'Whys?' – a book made out of this life, for this life. We are not far into its pages before we come upon Rebekah's 'family why?' (Genesis 25:22). And in no time we have the 'why?' of an old woman bereft, from Naomi, as she faces her young daughters-in-law (Ruth 1:11). And there is no missing the Psalmist's 'Why?' (Psalm 42:3). And when we turn to the New Testament, there are as many questions as ever – not the same ones, but others, implicit, or straightly asked. In every case, they come out of life, and are not artificially imposed upon it. It can't be otherwise – only by questioning can we find our way. That was Jesus's approach, and it must be ours.

'It is surprising', says Dr H. H. Farmer, speaking of many amongst us today, 'how often people will debate and argue all kinds of questions about Christ and Christianity, and *yet never really sit down and read the New Testament* with the sort of mind to which the New Testament claims to be able to speak, to the mind, that is, which is not seeking primarily to raise questions, but to find an answer to the urgent, and often desperate problems of how to manage life itself.' The real questions that arise are seldom academic, I find, but questions like: 'Why is life so short for some whom I love?' 'Why are the heavens as brass, sometimes when I pray?' 'Why do the godless so often succeed?'

We do not have all the answers, however many books we read, however long we have been Christians, however many theological classes we have attended. A reverence for truth is essential, an utter dependence on the character of God. The most difficult word that forms on our tongues is *'Why?'* Science, these days, can sometimes tell us 'How', but not often, if ever, *'Why'*. Many of our deepest experiences of life have to be *acted* out, before they can be argued out. Our Lord asked, 'Why?' on the Cross and received no answer in words. But He had faith enough in God, His Father, to surrender the highest He had, to the Highest He knew. 'Father', said He, 'into Thy hands I commit My Spirit!' *And He triumphed!*

So much suffering in this world of ours – as in His – seems to fall on the undeserving. It would not be so difficult, though difficult enough, to answer the question, 'Why, my God, why . . . ?' If we could see that suffering always followed some sort of reckless breaking of laws, of health rules, or deliberate ill-doing as a member of the community. But that's not how it is; and this baffles us.

In my wide reading of autobiography, I know of no cry more poignant than that of Damon Runyan, author, humorist, columnist of our day. He came to a point in his popular career where he found himself dying of cancer of the tongue. It was a grim discovery. 'When physical calamity falls', said he, 'the toughest thing for the victim is the feeling of resentment that it should have happened to him. "Why me?", he keeps asking himself dazedly. "Of all the millions of people around, why me?" It becomes like a pulse-beat – "Why me? Why me? Why me? Why me?" '

A lot depends on the spirit in which one approaches such an experience, of course. But one thing is plain – the good are not immune. If that were so, then all goodness would lose its essential quality – it would be something that paid handsomely in returns. But goodness isn't like that.

This, of course, is a little answer to a big question; it serves, somewhat, to blunt the painful edge of things. (We will push out a little further, in a later chapter on 'Why do we suffer?') We can say, in general terms at this stage, that man has marred the original purpose of God for this world that He created *and found good.* Over and over in the early word-picture of Creation, are the words : *'And God saw that it was good.'* (Genesis I : verses 4, 10, 12, 18, 21, 25, 31).

But we must be prepared, all too often, to leave question after question here unanswered. We can comfort ourselves by speaking of the long time God has in which to work, confidently declaring that divine love will redress issues in eternity. But it might be more helpful to own our human limitations, to utter our 'Why?' and trust ourselves, as our Master did, not to a spoken answer, but to *the unchanging character of God.* There is no greater meaning for us than the certainty of the first Easter, that *Jesus was vindicated.*

Still, our human questions rise. Joan Hutson, a young

Salvation Army Captain, whom I have come to know through writing, sent me lately a copy of her poem, 'The Unknown Dimension':

I stood beside the bed.
The small form, no longer restless,
Lay completely still;
No movement,
Nothing.
Time and eternity – the words hung suspended
Somewhere behind my dry, burning eyes.
The words held together but were poles apart;
Familiar, they meant nothing.
Time and eternity!
Where was she?
Was she asleep?
Not here;
Not in this still small form.
Then where?
Must she wait somewhere until the end of time,
Restless still?
That word 'eternity'.
My mind struggled to grasp the elusive dimension
On the brink of consciousness.
Eternity?
End of time – no time,
No past, no future – only now!
The ice of grief began to melt.
The wait would be mine,
Not hers!
The numbness, the searing pain of parting,
The wakeful nights – all mine.
A mystery, even now just beyond my grasp.
We would arrive together!
Not 'some now, others later' – that belongs to time.
I smiled. Then tears began to flow, and still I smiled;
For I was here, and she was there,
Gone to that unknown dimension in the heart of
   God –
And I was there as well.

You may some time walk through an old cemetery, and count the number of headstones that bear the words, *Thy Will be done!* These words lifted from the Lord's Prayer are, by so many people, deemed suitable for a moment of grief. Fewer graves are dug and tended nowadays, when cremation has become so widely accepted; but one still finds people lifting these words about the Will of God, for their newspaper death notices. Dr James Reid is uncomfortably near the truth when he says, 'Most people, when the Will of God is mentioned, feel a cold shadow creeping over them.'

Early in my student days, I found myself wondering about this. It was part of my training to spend several half-days a week accompanying the District Nurse on her rounds in the southern city of Christchurch. Apart from tending many sick and aged in their homes, any poor, broken body brought by the police to the Public Mortuary came under our care. A murder, suicide, or unexplained death, meant always for us an early morning call.

I shall never forget my first, my companion on that occasion a loved senior nurse. She had to tell me that our concern was the body of an old lady knocked down in the street the night before. She had been well-known for years in the city, as a favourite visitor at the hospital. (All this I gleaned in the few minutes it took to call at the hospital office for a key, and particulars. It appeared that the old lady's only son had been tragically wounded, and had been invalided home, sick in mind and body. In one of his 'turns' he had resisted his old mother, and had caused her to lose the sight of one eye.) For years, added Nurse, she had been obliged to 'keep him away', in an institution. Now, she had been knocked down in the street by a bicycle without a light, on her way to hospital for the evening visiting-hour. The simple facts were in themselves a shock – as was my first grim duty at the

Public Mortuary – but together nothing like the shock that came to my spirit when Nurse piously referred to the cause of our unhappy task, as *'the Will of God'*.

The Will of God? The words struck me – and I had no words. But I have thought about this unworthy use of those words again and again since. To get them straight, it has since seemed to me, is a very important thing in one's attitude to God. This is a painful issue on which one needs to be practical.

You remember, perhaps, a character – a very fine and sensitive character – in A. J. Cronin's *Keys of the Kingdom*. 'He entered the pro-cathedral, an echoing vastness of beauty and silence . . . Undaunted, he marched toward the high altar. There he knelt, and fiercely, with unshaken valour, prayed : "O Lord, *for once* – not Thy will, but mine, be done".'

Our Lord never once in His lifetime prayed a prayer of this nature; because He never once thought of God's Will as *a grief, rather a glory.* In setting the Will of the Father at the heart of the prayer He taught His followers, He was asking them to share the secret of His own life. 'My meat', said He [His very source of life and strength] 'is *to do the will of Him that sent* Me.' (John 4 :34). And He rejoiced in that. Again, on another occasion, He said : 'I seek not Mine own Will, *but the Will of the Father.*' (John 5 :30). Even within the dim shadows of Gethsemane's Garden, He prayed : 'Let this cup pass from Me, nevertheless not as I will, *but as Thou wilt.*' (Matthew 26 :39).

How strangely some of us interpret His spirit; at no time did He associate the Will of the Father exclusively with difficulty, despair or death. As Dr Robertson Nicoll wonderingly reminds us : 'He did not merely accept the Will of God, when it was brought to Him, and laid upon Him. Rather, *He went out to meet that loving Will*, and fell upon its neck and kissed it.' It is because so many of us so often fail to count on *the character of God*, that we blunder so badly. Lowell, the poet, knew better, and set us a good lead. Said he :

God is in all that liberates and lifts,
In all that humbles, sweetens and consoles.

So we might more truly put those words, 'Thy will be done!' over the birthplace of our maternity hospitals, our homes, kindergartens, schools, our playing-fields, youth clubs, churches, over concert halls, libraries, laboratories. The Will of God, as Jesus knew it, is to be identified with every good living thing, every piece of truth, every expression of justice and hope and joy. 'Some people pray this prayer', one has said, 'as if it is God's Will to take away babies.' But it is more truly expressed in the efforts of the United Nations Children's Fund. A little while back this was underlined by an old village priest in north-east Brazil. Asked if the efforts were worthwhile, he pointed to the bell on his church tower. Then he said simply, 'Once, it used to toll the death of a child three or four times a day. *Now* it rings only three or four times a month.'

When you and I – with countless other Christians the world around – learn to love, and to do the Will of God, with the consent of all our faculties and the resources of this modern age in which we live, that bell will not ring at all. Every such situation, where little children suffer and die needlessly, awaits the doing of the Father's Will. Every place of decision leading into action affecting others' lives, awaits the doing of the Father's Will. Every home – wherever situated, high or low, where money earned is spent for pots and pans, meals, books, clothes, holidays – awaits the doing of the Father's Will. And the same is true of every school, every church, every directors' boardroom, every piece of soil tilled for farm or garden, every factory, every workshop, every garage.

Let me rise each morning with these glorious words on my lips, *'Thy Will be done!'* For the Will of God is to be identified with life – in every one of its innumerable forms – not alone with death.

It often takes one a while to recognize this, to see, beyond one's own will and short-sightedness, where that Will lies. In a dramatic moment, early in my Christian experience, the words of Our Lord came to me : '*All power is given unto Me . . . Go ye . . . and lo, I am with you always, even unto the end of the world!*' (Matthew 28 : 18-20).

Nothing at the time seemed more clear – costly though it might be – than that I should spend my young life's energies as a missionary. So for six years at business I learned everything I could, with a correspondence course at night, everything that would help me in the Solomon Islands, the tropical part of 'the world' to which I believed I would be sent, since it was the one overseas field of my own Methodist Church. So everything I could read about it, I did; every missionary who spoke to us whilst on furlough, spoke to me – I was never missing; every new skill – first aid, half-soling shoes, elementary carpentry, cooking, public-speaking – was for my missionary life. I offered officially (with the commendation of my minister, who valued my experience as a youth-leader) first for training as a Deaconess of the Church. There, as a student for two years, I engaged in District Nursing in addition to my theological studies, with history, psychology, and English added; and with a period out with the Plunket Nurse devoted to baby-care. 'All this', I said to myself, 'will be useful later.'

Toward the end of my training, when the General Secretary of Foreign Missions came to a meal before going on to his evening meeting, I was invited to accompany him, which I did, thinking, 'Now is the time when he will tell me what the Board intends about my appointment.' *But he never uttered a word about it*, as we walked to and from the meeting! And I finished my training – with distinction, our Principal noted, as did the speaker at my valedictory service – but neither mentioned overseas missions.

I was sent, instead, to a back-country, pioneer charge of a group of churches in my own country – and nobody in authority has ever, to this day, spoken to me of service in the Solomon Islands, the special missions area of my New Zealand Church. Many parts of the world I have since visited, as speaker and writer, but I have never cast eyes on the Solomons, have never been asked to. From my two country appointments I was moved to a city mission, with broadcasting and social work as a constant charge, on to the writing of over sixty books that have led me to circle the earth by request several times. This has been my life-service – honoured by my church as the first woman Vice-President, representing its lay people; honoured by the Queen with the OBE, as recognition of what I have put into the long years.

Now that I write in these general terms it may seem that my early 'call', *Go ye into all the world!*, was a delusion. I always felt it to be so real. Now I wonder if it wasn't simply that I mis-interpreted those words as the Will of God for me, because of my limited experience at the time. I thought that the most exacting, most costly piece of Christian service I knew of, was to be mine – because I was ready to give myself utterly: *'Go ye into all the world . . . and lo, I am with you always!'* But isn't that, looking back, exactly what I have done? – through much travel, speaking in public places, and the writing of many books. My immense mail confirms it. Lately, when a reader – a Roman Catholic priest associated with a Canadian college in a university – wrote, I was moved when he concluded his letter, *'May God continue to bless your vocation as a writer!'* Understanding, as he does, the word 'vocation', I felt ready to dedicate myself anew, to 'go into all the world'.

16. WHO HAS A HEART THAT ENJOYS?

'You seem built to enjoy things,' said a listener a while back, when I finished a broadcast. My immediate answer was, 'But aren't we all?' Much of her surprise seemed to be in the fact that I broadcast as a religious person, on religious matters. Maybe she had not been as fortunate as I was, in stumbling on an old catechism, in the early stages of my search for God, which said, among other important things, 'Man's chief end is to glorify God, and to *enjoy* Him for ever.' My life would have lacked a great deal of colour without that word 'enjoy'. I hardly dared believe it at first; but after a time I found it confirmed in a letter Paul wrote to young Timothy. It added meaningfully to my conception of God. It said, *'God ... giveth us richly all things to enjoy.'* (I Timothy 6 : 17). I fell in love with that reality; and despite all manner of hindrances, I've never let it go. I knew already, in growing up, what it was to enjoy cool breath entering my lungs on a bright frosty morning; to enjoy the wind waving in soft grasses on the hillside; to enjoy the smell of white clover, as I ran across one of our fields by a shortcut. (The road in which our home stood was called 'Clover Road', and our farm afforded much to enjoy.) There were great trees along the road I travelled daily; new words full of beauty and meaning in the books I gathered for my eager mind; songs I shared with friends; jobs I did; plans I evolved. It was wonderful to think of God as the great giver of all these things. Borrowing the expression of one of my early-found heroes, that gay missionary spirit, Temple Gairdner, I constantly found myself saying with him, 'My heart is full of praise for God ... *I have claimed the heart that enjoys!'*

This, surely, is every Christian's right – though still, if one may judge from casual contacts, and dull countenances – this claim is not everywhere made. I actually heard these very words of Paul's misread in a Christian gathering, as 'God . . . giveth us all things richly to *endure*'. (Perhaps it was the reader's glasses, or the poor lighting where the company was gathered, or perhaps it was the set of his mind. I don't know.) But the word is 'enjoy', not 'endure'.

I have never myself been shy about enjoying things. Lately, I took time to weave some of them into a poem:

> I have found such joy in simple things —
> sun's early shafts on the still cool grass,
> a wash, and a kettle that sings,
> archipelagos of clouds that pass
> over trees tenanted by soft winds.
>
> Golden nut-brown toast with marmalade,
> a bell calling little ones to school,
> changing leaf patterns, deepening shade,
> a fluting blackbird in evening's cool,
> and a skein of duck flying homeward.
>
> So I bring my canticle of praise
> for these, and my room with lamp at dusk,
> for sweet rest after absorbing days,
> for many a kernel in the husk
> of printed books gathered through the years.
>
> R.F.S.

Our Master Himself enjoyed such things: grass and flowers; children at their games in the market-place, playing weddings and funerals; men at their daily work, mending nets under the wide sky; sowing seed — some falling on good ground, some on unpromising places. And He spoke of all these, so that they have come down to enrich us as we read the Gospels. He sat talking to Nicodemus, by night, on the house-top, the gentle wind stirring His garments; He came back from death's hold, before the first dew was off the grass in a garden, to speak a word of triumph to a loyal, loving Mary.

His very *enjoyment* of life raised problems in their acceptance of Him, for some. They could not believe that He was a genuine religious teacher — most known to them deported themselves with such solemn dignity; none of them thought of *enjoying* the world in which they found themselves. Many chose to live apart from their fellows, and had to be sought out in the desert, or in some hidden place of precious privacy. But Jesus mingled with the ordinary people – taking a meal here, another there, talking with many of no religious standing about the real things that concerned them as parents, builders, worshippers, the healthy along with the sick, and the anxious – some with whom many failed to talk, and only talked about. Some there were who had done business with Him, as the village carpenter, setting house foundations, fashioning yokes and chests, and they were familiar with His spirit. They had never found Him to pass off a shabby job, or to charge an unreasonable sum, or to show disrespect to a fellow craftsman. And they trusted Him – so that when He spoke of holy things He had learned from God, they listened. Occasionally, in the crowds, were sharp debaters from outside, ready to question His authority, His genuineness, His joy. And a few mingled with the crowds, who were pleased to argue about knowing His father and mother, and family. 'Is not this the carpenter's son?' they queried. 'Is not his mother called Mary? and his brethren, James and Joses, and Simon, and Judas? And his sisters, are they not all with us? Whence then hath this man all these things? And they were offended in him.' (Matthew 13:55-57).

He enjoyed health – and the physical stamina which supported it. No flabby-muscled, flat-chested, paleface was He : He couldn't have done the craftsman's job He did, had He been such, much less commanded the respect of tough fishermen; and He did. They became His friends – and friendship for Him was a deep, far-reaching, warm experience. He enjoyed fellowship with them; and He enjoyed the rich gifts of God which came to Him through His religion.

Paul – I learned, with some surprise – was in prison, when he wrote those beautiful words to young Timothy, 'God . . . giveth us richly all things to *enjoy*'. Centuries on, John Wesley's words to his fellow Christians who gathered about him, were, 'Every believer ought to *enjoy* life'. And some, in my day, have carried the secret still further forward. I have mentioned Temple Gairdner. In a collection of his letters, *W.H.T.G. to his friends*, one wrote, 'I have a vivid remembrance of one day when the College garden was what only an Oxford College garden in the summer sunshine can be, and he took my arm and said, "Let's watch the garden praising God!", and then began to chant in his strong, virile voice, *"O ye delphiniums, bless ye the Lord . . ."* And so on, right round the garden borders.'

Like Gairdner and his friends, the friend with whom I make home has often said to me, 'The thing I would miss most, were you suddenly to die, would be to have no one close to whom I could say, "Come, and look at this!" or "Listen a few minutes to this!"'

Enjoyment within the family is a very rich gift of God – one cooks well, and appetizing meals result; one gardens well, and even unpromising soil can be coaxed to yield fragrance and colour; one is a good reader-aloud, and the rich experience of other lives can be shared; one knows music, and can uncover hidden significances that might otherwise pass unnoticed.

And no words – Sunday by Sunday at worship – express one's gratitude for so much so well, as the General Thanksgiving : 'We bless Thee for our creation, preservation, and all the blessings of this life, but *above all* for Thine inestimable gift in the redemption of the world by our Lord Jesus Christ.' This is, in this world, God's richest gift ! 'new life in Christ, the hope of glory !'

17. IT'S EASY TO SAY, ISN'T IT?

Paul had a wide experience of life, and we can gain much from his writings. But he never rode on an escalator in a store, from floor to floor. Lately I visited a newly-opened one – and ascending pleasantly, past stand after stand, as each came into view, I thought of a striking thing he said in the first Christian century : *'The spiritual man is alive to all true values!'* (I Corinthians 2 : 15; Dr Goodspeed translates it.)

Life, of course, was very much simpler then. Even a hundred years ago, experts tell us, the average person's 'wants' were eighty-two – today, by the same reckoning, they are four-hundred-and-eighty-four! And what a variety!

In *Television and the Child* – the Himmelweit report on a commission set up to discover a child's view of modern society, and the effect of TV on that view – children were asked to describe the living-room of a rich family. One child put in two TV sets; another crowded in all the expensive objects she could think of – thick wall-to-wall carpet, TV, radiogram, chandelier, and a washing machine. Others, in turn, put in cocktail cabinets, huge mirrors, animal trophies, and rugs before a large fire burning beside a piano. Things! Things!

Children, from the very earliest age, absorb parents' values, and often without anything being said. 'Me', 'My', 'Mine', find an early place in a vocabulary.

The tyranny of things had already its hold upon many, before ever our modern newspaper advertisements, TV, radio, and seductively arranged displays added to the temptation. Long enough ago I came upon a word-picture in Sheila Kaye-Smith's novel, *Sussex Gorse*. It sketched in the stubborn fight of a farmer for things – a tract of gorse-land over against his farm, as his foremost desire. In the struggle, he sacrificed himself, his family, and the happiness they might have had together. In the end, he acquired what he had so long and single-mindedly set his heart on. But his words – honestly and stubbornly spoken, the last we hear from him – sound the death-knell of his spirit : 'I've won . . . I've won . . . *I've wanted a thing*, and I've got it . . . and when I die . . . well, I've lived so close to the earth all my days that I reckon I shan't be afraid to lie in it.'

But it's a sad story. By Paul's reckoning, he declared himself far from being 'a spiritual man . . . alive to all true values'. For *the thing* that he wanted so desperately, he sacrificed the finer qualities of the spirit – love, tenderness, joy. Everything costs something. But life is much more than things.

My friend Peter – broadcasting the other day – underlined this unforgettably in modern terms, and when I showed interest, he kindly handed me his script. His strong, attractive, virile voice rings through every word of it, and his on-going witness in the community, as a youngish minister, confirms it. 'When I first went to work in a professional office in the early 1950s, I had one ambition', said he, 'to get rid of my battered schoolboy satchel and acquire one of those smart business-like efficient-looking Gladstone bags. Everyone who looked as though he were anybody, carried one. Lawyers, accountants, executives . . . To my young eyes, that bag symbolized success, of the enterprising men at the top; and if I was to become a successful attorney, then it seemed proper for me to have one, too!

'I eventually got one – and though it's a long time ago now – I dare say it gave my self-esteem and ego a boost, as I carried it to and fro, until it dawned upon me it didn't mean a darn thing!

'I've still got that bag – very battered and marked now – not even a schoolboy would want it', added Peter.

'Anyway, the Gladstone bag has been superseded! There's a smart new model now of hard black vinyl, with strong steel edging and important looking locks . . . To stand in Queen Street, or catch the early morning plane to the capital, and see who's carrying this important-looking bag, is fascinating. For quite obviously, *we are* meant to be impressed by it. And I'm sure many men regard their briefcase as an outward symbol of the world we live in, of what our society regards as *important, wise* and *powerful* . . .

'And, of course, the papers and documents inside indicate thoughtful, high-powered, business expertise, progressive ideas. In short, the way our modern society gets things done, the way we control and manipulate things, the way we measure what is successful and enterprising, what is failure and futility.'

My friend went on to speak of the Cross, as the symbol of love, and life's other lasting values. And the words Paul spoke suddenly stood out as immensely relevant: *'The spiritual man is alive to all true values.'*

But things get loved, often, and people get used — instead of the other way round, which is the Kingdom's way of true values: with people loved, and things used. It often happens that relationships between some who should be close become severed, for the sake of things. Jesus found Himself questioned about such a situation. One asked: ' "Master, speak to my brother, that he divide the inheritance with me." And He said unto him: "Man, who made Me a judge or a divider over you?" And He said unto them, "Take heed, and beware of covetousness: for a man's life consisteth *not in the abundance of things* which he possesseth".' (Luke 12 : 13-15).

An abundance — however good the gathered things — can spell disaster, if not well handled. The leisurely Thames went on its way one morning not long ago, when I was ready to leave Abingdon to make my way to quiet Clifton Hampden. To a friend new in those parts, I said, 'Come with me, and we'll find some morning coffee.' And she did.

Morning sunshine, fine trees, and timbered and thatched cottages awaited us. I parked the car, and we walked the little distance that divided Oxfordshire and Berkshire, by way of the bridge with graceful arches. On the river bank, comfortably settled, was the old inn, The Barley Mow, made famous by Jerome K. Jerome's *Three Men in a Boat*, when they tied up at the landing stage near by. Sitting over our coffee, I recalled their dilemma, arising out of the possession of things. Their minds on the trip they meant to make up the river, they started by making a list. But all was not as simple as they supposed. 'It was clear that the upper reaches of the Thames would not allow the navigation of a boat sufficiently large *for the things* we had set down as indispensable', said Jerome, 'so we tore up the list and looked at one another. George said, "You know, we're on the wrong tack altogether. We must not think of the things we could do with, *but only of the things we can't do without*".'

And here is the dual test, not only the worthwhileness of things, but the abundance of them. The spiritual man and woman have to mind these issues all the time.

Travelling in America with a business friend, I have never forgotten one of the striking statements thrown up in his talk. 'In this country, in this thing-centred century, a baby is born every twelve seconds, but a car every *five* seconds.' And in that saying, I saw people and things as they exist in juxtaposition. In the main, people are more difficult to deal with than things – though *they* are difficult enough. Our homes, shops and factories today are full of things. Nothing must last too long; we have coined the horrible word 'obsolescence' to match our hunger for something new all the time, something brighter and better. Our choices merge on covetousness, and our precious free lives become cluttered. Says one, 'I worship my car, a Jaguar. It establishes me among my business associates. All my spare time belongs to it. To pass a soft cloth over its pristine loveliness is a satisfying ritual.' 'I worship my house', says another. 'It's in a nice locality. It proclaims the fact that I've married well.' 'I worship my "telly",' says yet another. 'I can't think whatever I did with my long evenings before I had it – a colour one, too.'

We talk about 'the cost of things'; but *the cost of any one thing* is the amount of life it requires to be exchanged for it, immediately, or in the long run. Yearning for things, paying for things, living smothered with things, is the thumbnail sketch of many of us today.

Little children – before we spoil them with our adult

values – are not like this. I saw it when I helped with a Christmas tree, from which each little one present got a gift. I heard one mother after another whisper when a child's turn came to choose, 'Take the big ball', or 'Take the big doll' – mindful of the cost of each. And a child's first choice was often a tiny doll in bed in a match-box; or a pocket-knife, costing little in the market. Again, I saw these values when a child came on a visit to our home just before Christmas – my friend's little great-niece, four years old. Asked, 'What are you going to get from Father Christmas?' her answer was, 'A walkie-talkie doll – *or a tooth-brush* !' I wonder if this isn't close to what Our Lord had in mind when He talked about having the heart of a child? Values have really nothing to do with price-labels.

We are so modern, so sophisticated. Much is to be gained from living in this twentieth century – *and a lot to be lost in our handling of it.*

18. IS ANYTHING GAINED BY GOING TO CHURCH?

We claim to enter the fullest meaning of intercession, adoration, fellowship within the Church. Some question our claim. This may be because the word 'Church' is so ambiguous. We speak of a certain *sacred building*, known to us, as the church. But we use the same word, quite correctly, to describe *the company* worshipping therein; again, of *a union of such believers*, such as The Church of Scotland, for instance; and we use the same word of *the whole number of believers now living* – as the Christian Church of today; and extending its use further still, *as the whole body of believers ever* – past, present, and to come. In the Apostles' Creed we are each taught : 'I believe in the Holy Catholic Church' – here the word 'catholic' means 'the world-wide, whole universal Church of Christ'. *The Visible Church* is made up of those of us avowed disciples now living; *the Church Triumphant* is made up of those who have finished their spiritual battle; *the Invisible Church* includes the sainted dead; *the Church Militant* is the Church now on earth. Jesus taught that a confession of faith in Himself should be the tie binding Church members. To make it possible for them to discharge a world-embracing mission, He promised that as they went out to share His Gospel in all places, He would be as close to them as they had ever known Him – His *seen* presence, after His ascension, become *unseen* (Matthew 28 : 19-20). Many first come to realize this within the sacred building we call 'the church'.

My first editor, Dr Leslie Church, was a gracious person in all that he said and did – discussing one's new book; preaching; broadcasting; writing. On my several visits to London, he became my friend. But it wasn't till his premature death that I learned how he first became a Christian, and a member of the Church. His father was a Methodist minister, the Reverend Frederick Church. Sometimes when he went to lead worship, young Leslie went with him. Like the rest of us, they shared good times, and grey times when it seemed that not much, if anything, of interest was happening. But one night, at Richmond Road Church – rapidly becoming a down-town building – the service was different. To the devoted preacher it seemed usual enough. But later, when they got home and he was in his study looking back over the day's work, his young son entered, asking: 'Dad, can I speak to you?' 'Yes, Leslie.' 'Dad', went on the young fellow, 'when you were preaching tonight, I gave myself to Christ!' Never had joy, tears and wonder so mingled in that loved father's experience. He walked always a little humbler after that, and yet a little taller.

Age has nothing to do with this reality. I like the way Alfred Noyes, poet and editor, recognized this. Said he, of his father in old age, 'If ever I had any doubts about the fundamental realities of religion, they would always be dispelled by one memory – the light upon my father's face as he came back from early Communion.'

I was invited back to a city Mission Church a little while ago, as guest preacher at its hundred-and-twenty-fifth anniversary. Forty-five years earlier I had served there as a young deaconess. The old buildings – shabby in my day – had been replaced by a beautiful chapel, standing beside a fine aspiring city block. And there were other changes, not least the well-clad congregation in this affluent society, very different from the shabby front which was the best we could manage in those hard times of unemployment created by a country-wide economic depression.

Present at our recent worship was one returned hundreds of miles for the occasion, who said to me, when there was a chance to talk during a bountiful lunch, 'I remember when I first met you. You were on your knees in one of the old classrooms. But you weren't praying – though you did a good deal of that, too, in those days, as I came to know – you were half-soling men's boots, so that they could go to Labour Camps in the country.' 'Yes!'

And our worship spread out into other service, too. Lacking the modern term 'counselling', we talked over personal problems as they arose, as trusted friends. We visited homes, hospitals, courts and prisons, and ran week-night choir-practices, and week-day jumble sales, and Mothers' Meetings. We weren't quite so polished in our worship – but there was unquestioned reality about it.

I recalled an old grandmother, who one day at the Mothers' Meeting volunteered to sing a solo. Accepting her offer, I said, 'Yes, of course . . . we'd love it.' At the appointed time, she took up her place out in front; but she didn't begin. Presently, explaining this, she said, 'Sister, I'll have to sing something I know by heart – *I've come without me specs.*' 'That will be all right', I assured her, 'sing something you know.' But still she stood – and we waited. Then out came her excuse for delay, 'I'm sorry, Sister, it won't be as good as it usually is – I've come without me teeth; they were hurting me.' A titter went round; but only momentarily. Next, there was a hushed, respectful silence, as that old soul stood – without specs, without teeth – and sang for us all three verses of 'Blessed Assurance, Jesus is mine!' And meant it! It was an impressive witness, especially to those of us who chanced to know her background.

There is no livelier book in the world than the New Testament book of Acts – and no livelier passage in it than that which recalls Christ's challenge to His followers, then, and for all times. Said He, 'Ye shall be *witnesses* unto Me, both in Jerusalem [where they were just then], in all Judea [the next place out] and in Samaria [further still from base] and unto the uttermost part of the earth!' (Acts 1 :8). Its emphasis lay on a definite *beginning*, and *expansion*! 'In the Gospels', as an Indian explained to Dr John Foster, 'it was Jesus, His works and His suffering. In the Acts . . . *the Church continued* where He left off at His death. Therefore', said the new disciple, 'I must belong to the Church that carries on the life of Christ.'

The word for *witness* in that stirring passage in Acts, and the word for *martyr*, were the same : *martus.* A witness had to be ready to face up to whatever his worship demanded. And those two words were intermingled at a very costly level in the early centuries. And they are today, within the Church in many parts of the world. In Russia, many Christians languish in prisons – many of them without trial. And in other parts also.

From the very start of the story told in Acts, men and women worshipped Jesus – their church-going a stimulus, not a substitute, for action. And where life counts in the world, these things are still true; the Acts of the Apostles underlines these values till the end of Time. Dr Berkhof, of the Netherlands, stressed this, in addressing the World Council of Churches : 'A preaching church without a life of love and mercy', said he, 'has no winning power. *Witness* without service is empty; service without *witness* is dumb.'

This glorious balance worried Celsus, the second-century philosopher. Of the early Christians, and their life in the Church – though they had at that time no special buildings that could be called 'churches' – 'This infection,' said he, 'has spread through cities, villages, and country districts.' Infection indeed ! Their basic witness belongs to Christian living. It expresses itself, starting in what adds up to your 'Jerusalem', and mine, where we are – in the home, the office, the university, in the street. And going out to our 'Judea', the next place where we circulate, worship and serve; and out to our 'Samaria', further still, eventually taking in the world and its 'uttermost parts'. It is in response to the charge delivered by our Risen Lord to the young amongst us; to those of us middle-aged, aged, bearing the burden of building, administering, and sustaining the Church's worship and witness to the end of Time, here.

Some unfortunately – especially young folk – are inclined, these days, to get these essentials back to front. They want to set the world right, to go out into action first, to run clubs, to serve on committees, to prepare manifestoes on social and political issues of the day, to attend world conferences. All these are doubtless important – and may be called 'witnessing'; *but unless we take time for church attendance – for regular worship – when we are running so hard, we will soon find ourselves less aware of Christ, short of power, even lacking divine purpose amidst our fellows.*

Is anything gained by going to church?

The word 'worship' comes to us from the same root as 'worth', 'worthy' and 'worthwhile'. And no other 'gathering together', club, society anywhere on this earth, exists, as does the Church, to set this uppermost. Only the Church can teach us to worship. Sensing the depth of this miracle, I find my thoughts running to Christians as dissimilar as Barbara Ward, Billy Graham, John Betjeman, Mother Teresa, the Archbishop of Canterbury, the Leader of the Society of Friends, Trevor Huddlestone, the President of the Methodist Conference, the Salvation Army officer I know best, Dr J. S. Stewart of the Church of Scotland, not forgetting humble souls isolated in parts where no church worship is possible, in Chinese cities, in Russia, where secular authority forbids it, but countless men and women hold strongly to the faith. These and others make up the Church in the world as Our Lord sees it, loves it, and uses it. Their views may differ at many points, their creeds be clothed in different terms of devotion, their mode of service be dissimilar; but I am not barred from acknowledging any one of these as my fellow Christian.

Some of us worship in dignified and comfortable city or suburban churches; some in simple country buildings, the only beauty within, a bunch of flowers from some worshipper's garden; some of us worship in mission huts made of local palmleaf; some in Quaker Meeting Houses; some in immense and glorious cathedrals built and beautified through the centuries. Some are satisfied with simple hymns, loved of their parents before them; some rejoice in stately masses; some hush their spirits with the aid of gracious and gifted choirs.

When we worship God, we recognize in Him, and His revelation within man's earth story, the words of the prophets, and the life, death, and rising-again of our Lord – values called 'everlasting'. And we identify ourselves with His Will in the world we know; and we offer our total faculties, funds of energy, money, and experience, to serve His Kingdom, where we are, and progressively out 'to the ends of the earth'. We come tired, to be refreshed; doubting at some point or other, to be reassured;

world-stained, slipping at some point or other in our human relationships, needing to be forgiven; uncertain of our next step, needing to be guided, and sustained; feeling a good deal on our own, needing to know ourselves, in reality, part of a great company of witnesses of all time, and now, in earth and in heaven. Archbishop William Temple's glorious summing-up still excites me, and I have not found this greatest human experience set down more memorably : '*To worship* is to quicken the conscience by the holiness of God, to feed the mind with the truth of God, to purge the imagination by the beauty of God, to open the heart to the love of God, and to devote the will to the purpose of God.'

And here we are back at witnessing – and set in its proper place, worship first, and then all the acceptance of what opportunities the day brings. And soon, adoration, which is the heart of worship, breaks from us in all sorts of places, and at all manner of times – taking into our open hands the Bread and the Wine; rising to share in a loved, triumphant hymn; seeing a new significance in familiar words of Scripture; coming suddenly on the way home upon a swathe of Spring flowers of God's creation; finding beauty and joy in the movements of a child; sharing a piece of hospital news about a friend's recovery; or seeing, like Alfred Noyes, the glow on another's face, coming from Communion.

Denomination has little or nothing to do with it. 'The Church exists by Mission', says Brunner, the distinguished modern scholar, 'as fire exists by burning.' And nationality has little, if anything, to do with it. I once had the privilege of leading an international camp at morning worship for several weeks, where – belonging to thirteen nationalities – we were as one. When we came to the Lord's Prayer, we each said it in her own tongue, which was impressive.

And physical, and economic, need has little, if anything, to do with it. I once worshipped, on the World Day of Prayer, in a finely carpeted, stained-glassed church in New York; and not long afterwards, on my travels, tried to share a hymnbook with a worshipper next to me – a leper woman, in a little settlement church away in the north of Australia, an aborigine. I had to hold the book for both of us, because she had lost both hands to the dread disease. But we were, in each of these experiences, Christians at worship.

Some of the finest characters to be met with anywhere are members of the Church; some of the most gracious; some of the most courageous; some of the most delightful; the most able, and widely informed.

And it must be admitted that there are others – dull people, little-minded people, critical people, who somehow haven't yet caught hold of the Spirit of Jesus, with its love, joy, peace, long-suffering, gentleness, goodness, faith, and all the other lovely qualities exhibited by our Master.

The Church, of course, is not – and never has been – a privileged company of perfect characters. But stay outside the Church, and you miss much!

19. HOW CAN ONE GROW WITHOUT THIS ADVENTURE?

Stepping out into the street one morning lately, I over-took a small boy, about eight or nine, I suppose he would be. Sharing the early sunshine, I broke the silence between us : 'This is a lovely morning, isn't it? I hope you've had a happy holiday.' To my surprise, he replied : 'Well, no, I haven't.' 'Oh, how was that?' I queried, taken aback. 'Well,' said he, now walking beside me, 'at the end of last term, I became a "book-worm". And I was looking for-ward to the holidays, for a good read. But the family got a new car – and every day they wanted to go out. And I had to go, too – for a picnic, or a visit to somebody. So I didn't get my long read.'

I expressed sympathy as best I could. 'I understand,' said I, 'because I'm a "book-worm", too. I read lots of the loveliest books – and I *write* books, too. Some day, when you are older,' I made an effort to reassure him, 'you'll get to know the secret of using every odd bit of time.'

As we parted at the top of our street, I called after him, 'Goodbye ! *And good reading!*' I hope we meet again.

No delight of my life, since I was his age, has been more constant than the power to read. When I fashioned my large anthology, *Delight Upon Delight* – a lovely title, that – I dedicated it : 'In gratitude to those who taught me to read, and have now gone upon their way, G. and H.' Those initials belong to my father and mother, George and Hilda. Others, in due time, helped me to dig into English grammar for the kernel at its heart, and to cut a trail for myself through the thickets of literature.

But for years, I must admit, I read my Bible *as a task enjoined*, never *as a delight to be enjoyed*. Then for twenty-four pence, I bought a book by one unknown to me at the time, Anthony Deane, called surprisingly, *How to Enjoy the Bible*. I'd never thought of anyone 'enjoying' the Bible. My difficulty lay largely in the fact that I had not dreamed that it was not a book – *but a library*. I started to read it, as any other book, from the beginning on; and after Genesis, and Exodus, got stuck. No wonder I made no headway – whoever heard of anyone reading 'a library', beginning just inside the door, as I started just inside the front cover of my Bible? (I hope my little 'bookworm' will not run into this difficulty – he need not, for there are any number of paperback guides these days, to give him a start.) He can learn there that the Bible is not a book of science, but belongs to the childhood of the race. It is also essential to know that it is written in many types of writing, and on a progressive structure, so that the morals of the people, their social and national behaviour, gradually rise through the centuries. In time, his reading will bring him to the glories of the New Testament with its emphasis of love, truth and joy. 'From start to finish', as Dr Roger Pilkington of our day sums up, 'this series of books is about *the nature of God*, and one should not be sidetracked by its genealogies, the primitive astronomy, the blood-curdling murders, and the competitive polygamy in some of the Old Testament items.' The Bible is, above all, a religious book, enriching all our life with its wide-embracing interests, its honesty, its grace of diction.

The Bible, in the Authorized Version, with which we are most of us first familiar, one speaks of as, 'The best words of the best period of English, in the best order.' And though some words in that Version of 1611 have now changed their meaning, it is this Version that led Anthony Deane to speak of 'enjoying' the Bible. 'Train yourself', he said, 'not merely to feel in a general way the Bible's literary charm, but to notice in detail how that charm is gained. What has made the wording of this sentence so extraordinarily effective? What gives that paragraph its perfection of rhythm? What were the methods of those who made this wonderful English? When we pass, in short, from saying: "How fine this is!" to asking, "*Why* is this so fine?", we put ourselves in the way of acquiring a new interest, of finding a new and inexhaustible pleasure in our reading. *It will not lessen other and deeper pleasures* . . . Perhaps', he adds, 'the simplest beginning is to notice how skilfully the translators chose their words from our rich vocabulary. They prefer, for the most part, *short words*. They know the tranquil effect given by a flow of monosyllables. *"Blessed are the pure in heart, for they shall see God"* – and in Ruth, that idyll of the harvest-field, how exactly the wording of this sentence matches the setting, enhances its simple grace : *"The Lord do so to me, and more also, if aught but death part me and thee"* – seventeen words, and only eighteen syllables. Try the result of re-casting that in longer words, and observe how its tender charm is marred ! But no less well did those translators know how to employ sonorous Latinisms when a loftier diction was in better accord with the sense : *"Now unto the King eternal, immortal, invisible . . ."* and again, *"This corruption shall put on incorruption, and this mortal shall put on immortality . . ."* Is not that a triumph of art? But one might write chapters to praise these translators' astounding skill, alike in their choice of words and their control of rhythm. That rhythm you hear sometimes in a monotonous pulsing throb of lamentation : *"Ye daughters of Israel, weep over Saul, who clothed you in scarlet, with other delights"* – and sometimes in a glorious ascent to a climax of triumphant faith : *"Neither death, nor life, nor angels, nor principalities, nor powers, nor things present, nor things to come, nor height, nor depth, nor any other creature, shall be able to separate us from the love of God, which is in Christ Jesus our Lord."* '

But, of course, our English Bible's unmatched felicity of style is not the main thing – it is a book given by God, to bring us closer to God. Many of its phrases have slid into our common speech. We speak of 'the signs of the times'; 'a thorn in the flesh'; 'filthy lucre'; 'in season and out of season'; 'wars and rumours of wars'; and countless others, some of the loveliest we know – 'the labour of love'; 'strength of the hills'; 'honour to whom honour is due'; 'mine own familiar friend'; 'hoping against hope'.

It is true, in this Authorized Version many words have lived to puzzle us modern readers. Some of the most obvious are worth listing. The word 'prevent' means to

us to stop, or hinder; but when the Authorized Version
was given to the world, meant 'to go before'. In those
days, when a king, prince, or famous traveller went on
his way, always a servant went ahead as the day wore on,
to prepare lodging for the night – and when it was ready,
came out to meet his master coming in. So the Revised
Standard Version renders the Authorized Version of
Psalm 19 :8, instead of 'Let Thy tender mercies prevent us
. . .' which is puzzling; 'Let Thy compassion come speedily
to meet us'. And when the A.V. wrote : 'Who shall *let* it?'
of a certain issue, it did not mean, 'who shall allow it', but
'who shall hinder it?'; and when it said '*ye allow* the
deeds of your fathers', it did not mean, 'you permit them',
but 'you approve of them'. In 1611, '*coasts*' were bound-
aries, but not necessarily made by the sea; and the word
'*lust*' meant strong desire, not necessarily anything of a
sexual nature; and to '*comfort*' meant to strengthen – so
that 'Comfort ye, comfort ye, my people', had nothing to
do with the idea of cushions or soft words. (In one section
of the famous Bayeux Tapestry, at the end of a line of
soldiers, stands a bishop with a sword – directed to the
rump of the man just before him – and underneath are
the words : 'The Bishop *comforteth* his soldiers'! Years
on, Francis Asbury, father of the American Methodist
Church, finished an entry in his famous *Journal*, with
the words, 'Our Conference ended on Friday with a
comfortable intercession'. '*Cunning*' is another old word
that has completely changed. The Psalmist cried : 'If I
forget thee, O Jerusalem, let my right hand forget her
cunning.' But the word is not at all the word we meet in
our modern detective-yarn – its Bible meaning is 'skill'.

We are fortunate to have available today – thanks to
devoted modern scholars – many translations using our
own tongue. Truth, of course, is an on-going reality,
however words change. Modern archaeological discoveries
are also constantly throwing fresh light on our Bible
reading. Many things in our life change – but not at
heart cruelty, greed, fear, jealousy, pride; they remain
as ever – and on the other hand, love, friendship, kindness,
hope. Says Dr Harry Fosdick strikingly : 'We should put

Ruth's sickle in a museum, for we have vast machines which storm across the prairie and do the work of a thousand men : but Ruth, in her loyalty to her mother-in-law, would put us to shame. (*We have improved on Ruth's sickle, but have we improved on Ruth?*)'

My favourite modern translation is the Revised Standard Version, which not only clarifies the content, but carries forward for one a measure of literary charm that it would be a pity to lose. I keep it handy as I read my treasured Authorized Version – and on a shelf nearby, a number of others. Susan Langer is right : 'Language is, without a doubt, the most momentous and at the same time the most mysterious product of the human mind. Between the clearest animal call of love or warning or anger, and a man's least trivial word, there lies a whole day of Creation – or in a modern phrase, a whole chapter of evolution.'

Visiting Portrush, in Northern Ireland, in the course of a lecture tour for my publishers, a friend took me to meet an old 'book-worm'. He kept a little second-hand book-shop – so whatever he had lacked in youth was more than made up for. I was excited by his collection of books, taking up every inch of every shelf – even to volumes stacked on the steps of the stairs. Such good talk we shared ! And when it was time to go, I came away with a charming sentence from his rich heart : '*I never was at the schools – but I was much with the scholars!*' So his growing up was rich !

I was more fortunate, a generation or two later, as is my little 'book-worm' of today, stepping with me up our street. This is a rich time to be a reader and never a day goes by, but I give thanks to God for it. On holiday myself a little while ago, I wrote :

> Hours out of doors are now vanishing
>   like fluff of a dandelion-clock,
> Cicadas singing the requiem of Summer;
> One's garnering to carry into Autumn
>   a great sheaf of lovely things

How can one grow without this adventure?

For the days when blunt rain falls,
    friendly pines groan
And no living thing, meanwhile, is on
    speaking-terms with the sun.

But in the country here, there is always
    a late valley train
Chuffing its slender way beyond the
    range of hearing,
A dog turning in his guardianship, as I
    latch the door, for the fire
And a good, long read – pausing now and again
    to crack a word,
to get at its sweet kernel.

R.F.S.

Stewardship, as Christians understand it, is something more than wheedling money out of unwilling pockets. Though it may involve money, it covers the whole of one's person and possessions.

A steward, in New Testament times, was entrusted with the management of an estate, or a household. Even so, he was still a servant as far as his master was concerned. Neither personal power, nor prestige was allowed to get in the way.

Jesus lifted up this well-known relationship, and made of it an even lovelier thing. His emphasis was not on plebeian servility, but on privilege. I grasped this, with wonder, when first called to speak in public. I shall never forget that evening — so shy I was, at sixteen. My mother and many friends were in the little chapel that night, to support me. I was required to base my remarks on a text, and I chose Luke 12:48; and was carried away by the fairness of it. *'Unto whomsoever much is given, of him shall be much required.'* It's a long time ago now, and I can't recall what I said, but that idea of stewardship has been precious in my sight ever since. At that time, I saw it embraced my youthfulness, my abilities, and possessions; these seemed small gifts in return for God's wonderful gifts of creation, and reconciliation. To these, up through the years, in my home, my church, in service, in friendship, and travel, immensely more has been added — but my first stewardship text stands. *It turns, not on how many of my good gifts I might give to God, but on how many of God's good gifts I might keep for myself.* Happily, there have always been some great spirits who have seen the matter clearly — that the whole of life is a sacred trust — and they have given many of us a lead.

The distinguished and loved master of the cello, Pablo Casals, liked to speak to his young players on this issue. 'Don't be vain because you happen to have talent,' he

would say. 'You are not responsible for that : it was not
your doing. What *you do* with your talent is what matters.'
He was not a preacher, but he saw clearly this principle
of stewardship. And what he laid before his loved young
students, he acknowledged in his own day-to-day responsiveness.

Fritz Kreisler, another great artist of our day, used
actually to make use of the term 'steward'. Speaking once,
when praised for his personal gifts, he said, 'I was born
with music in my soul.' Then he went on to elaborate his
meaning, and to bring out his wife's lovely co-operation
toward a like understanding, when reference was made to
those many whom they had helped by their monetary
generosity. 'People do no seem to understand,' Kreisler
went on, 'just why we do not feel that we have any right
to spend money carelessly. They do not understand the
spiritual philosophy that is at the back of it. Therefore
they think we are temperamental or queer. It is very
simple : *we feel that we are stewards* both of my talent,
and of the money that comes to us from that talent. It is
God's gift, and we are its stewards. Why do people not
understand that all things belong to God?'

There are a great many motives for giving, and serving
– but this is supreme. It comes to us as an intrinsic part
of our Christian faith.

In most churches I know of, these days, stewardship
campaigns are held at regular times every three or four
years. These are designed to bring – especially to new
members – information and encouragement to give. Some
have a deep-rooted dislike of anyone knowing how much
they give, and welcome the personal freedom of choice
and respectful secrecy with which the matter is handled.
Some elect to tithe – promising a tenth of their income –
to the on-going ministry, missionary and compassionate
work of the church. This way, a lively congregation is able
to plan, knowing ahead from year to year, at least what
its guaranteed minimum resources are.

Not that Christian stewardship is limited to money –
far from it. It reaches out to involve our individual and
corporate care of the land, and all the natural resources

God has entrusted to us. 'The land', we are taught, 'is the Lord's – not the landlord's.' Scientific research has shown us many parts of the world where successive generations of nomadic farmers have destroyed precious resources. The Sahara has not always been desert; the Dust Bowl of America has come to exhaustion through ignorance, and the exploitation of greed; so that today we have, in many parts, a hungry world. Added to this we have, in many parts, limited cultivable land, resulting in an unbalanced diet and malnutrition. It has been estimated that an average of two-point-five acres of arable land are necessary to produce an adequate diet for each individual. Even so, all manner of variables, affecting the yield, have to be taken into account – climate, fertility, and such like.

And more important in our stewardship, is our readiness to share. I set this down in a poem, that I titled 'Bread on the Table'. Two-thirds of this world's people go to bed hungry, and waken with greater hunger in the morning. I live in a favoured land :

Here, morning breaks as the world's first morning,
The lark on high spills her silver coins of song.
We of the earth cannot live by bread alone,
Nor can we live without it long.
So a furrow is turned by honest plough,
And good seed flung into the earth;
Rain follows sun in slender spears
Till thin tassels spring to birth.

Nothing of God's giving is so golden crusted,
Nothing so sweet to taste and need as bread,
Save that our brother afar faints for it –
Bread tilled for, sown and harvested.
We would not begrudge nectar to the tipsy bee
Winging from flower to flower the long day through;
Our grievous fault is that we withhold this hour
Bread from our brother who knows hunger, too.

                                                      R.F.S.

And we have to do something about it – individually

and collectively. Once, it took months even to hear about the hungry, the ill-clad, but not now – this air age has changed all that. A short flight away is Asia – with 65 per cent of this great hungry world's teeming population. And there are, over all, millions of refugees, many of them illiterates, not knowing what is really happening to them, or why. And every time any country or state makes war, the dread problem is multiplied. Every time we look at a TV picture of their plight, brought right into our homes; every time the newspaper carries horrifying headlines; every time young men and women in our midst are stirred to give their skills, in service overseas – the problem becomes more relevant. It is bound up for us with the stewardship of the soil – for those of us who are farmers, merchants, shopkeepers – it is bound up with the erosion of good, rich hillsides, with the production and distribution of new types of seed, with effective tools, and the desire for economic justice.

It is not easy, but for Christians it is essential, since we pray: 'Our Father . . . give us this day our daily bread' . . . *Our* Father, *our* bread. All this is tied up with our stewardship, and must be. This way, the World Council of Churches is able to report back to our little congregation that in a single twelve-month, it has distributed some twenty-six thousand tons of food, clothing and medical supplies, established new homes for more than nineteen thousand refugees; sent one-and-a-half million dollars in cash for emergency help to victims of floods, earthquakes, fires and famine; and provided more than six million dollars for Inter-Church and Inter-Mission Aid projects – all this without any political or ecclesiastical, denominational tags attached.

Stewardship can't start too soon, or stretch too far. It is a moving experience to hear young people, newly come to faith, singing one by one:

> Nought that I have my own I call,
>   I hold it for the Giver:
> My heart, my strength, my life, my all
>   Are His, and His for ever!

21. WHAT IS LIFE WITHOUT LEISURE?

If there was ever a period when one thing happened at a time, it must have been long, long ago. Certainly, it was not in Palestine, in our Master's day. This came to me first as a great surprise, when – hard-pressed, and longing for leisure – I read a New Testament passage I had passed over many a time.

Nobody, I realized, ever got more into earthly days and nights; again and again the record was concerned with crowds that gathered about Jesus, and the claims they made on Him. His disciples were involved, too, of course. None of the distances was too great to attempt on foot; and the people followed, for preaching and healing. Neither the dustiness of the paths from place to place, nor the fierce heat of the sun deterred them. Crowds even pushed into houses where the Master was known to be – a woman with her secret, to wipe His feet free of her tears, during a meal; a sick fellow, carried on his pallet by four friends, let down through the roof, for healing; professional mourners shattering the quiet privacy of a home, when it was rumoured the little daughter of Jairus had died. And so His ministry continued endlessly – here a beggar waiting by the roadside, there a man up a tree, lest he should be deprived of the chance to see Him; there a pathetic leper, overlooking the law forbidding him to draw near; there, a noisy citizen; with sharp-tongued scribes and Pharisees, watching for a chance to undermine His authority, never far away. In Jerusalem it was liable to be even more exacting, with greater crowds, the heat in the narrow streets, the suspicious designs of the religious leaders, bolder on their own ground.

Each day began for Him before dawn – His only chance to get away into a place for prayer; ending often – as with Nicodemus, a ruler of the Jews, on the darkened rooftop under the stars, the night winds stirring.

Someone, in our day, has endeavoured to list His every

meeting mentioned in the New Testament records – and
the length of each – but that is to assume that His total
private and public life is recorded, no meeting omitted.
One cannot claim that much for the Gospel scribes. There
may well have been occasions that He alone could tell
about – as in the case of the Temptations in the Wilder-
ness. (Nobody else was there; had He not chosen to speak
of those happenings, we should never have known a thing
about them.)

If it comes to the point, we can never tell how long
it took Him to tell any one of His famous parables – nor
do we know whether He told them more than once. That
seems likely, judging by what I know of itinerant speakers.
We are told of one interruption as He went upon His way
– the raising to life of the only son of the distraught
widow of Nainm, as the burial cortège wound its way –
but did this sort of interruption not occur on other
occasions? And there was the continual need to train His
chosen disciples – men so dissimilar, with many rough edges
to rub off, many queries to answer. Whatever opportunities
presented themselves as they trudged from place to place
(they couldn't have been many, because the crowds were
so pressing) and night-hours around the camp-fire, must
have been the time for that.

No wonder we have a recorded word about leisure,
amidst so much activity. Mark found room for it in his
little Gospel, and how glad you and I ought to be to find
it there. It helps us with our scale of values. Not only
was the Master so human as to appreciate His own daily
needs; but He knew as deeply those of His disciples.
Against the exacting background, when His men had been
away on a set task, Mark says : 'They gathered themselves
together unto Jesus, and told Him all things, both what
they had done, and what they had taught.' (One can
imagine it all tumbling out; but that done, Jesus could see
tired bodies before Him, tired minds, tired spirits. As a
sensitive Master, He knew well what should be next on
the programme, for all that it had been exciting, and they
were ready to undertake as much again.) 'Said He unto
them', Mark records, ' "*Come ye yourselves apart into a*

deserted place, and rest a while." For there were many coming and going, and they had no leisure so much as to eat.' (Mark 6 :31).

We can understand the situation – we too have known times when the pressure of things, of people, has offered us 'no leisure so much as to eat'. Our needs then have been exactly those of the disciples – a quiet place where we could recover our spent selves; reconsider our over-all purposes; rest ourselves in the eternal refreshment of God.

It sometimes happens that we are so foolish that we do not accept the ministry of the quiet place – we even grow proud of our busyness. Described as 'thin, kind, and always in a hurry', a certain vicar's wife of whom I heard in the Cotswolds, came to be known as 'the galloping hair-pin'! It seems she knew the bustle and hustle that many of us know, the demands of people and situations – but she had not happened on the secret of physical, mental and spiritual renewal underlined by Our Lord. And that was a loss. It changed the quality of her service – and may well shorten its length. I would have thought that as a Christian woman, and living in the beautiful, peaceful Cotswolds, she might have marked out at least one place for retreat.

Before I travelled in the East, I had little idea of its life – Bible pictures, with sunny skies, the people comfortably clad, walking without knowledge of the engine-motor-speed we know, look so leisurely. But now I know life there can be otherwise – an Eastern market can be full of tensions. And because his life was not removed from the day's ordinary comings and goings, I find the Psalmist's secret, with which Our Lord was familiar. (Psalm 131 :2; R.S.V.) It was so gloriously positive. Said he : 'I have calmed and *quieted my soul*.'

And you and I must somehow discover ways to do the same. We must achieve a quiet of mind and spirit which is something more than mere absence of noise and people. Those of us fortunate enough to live deep in the country may be able to escape into quiet more easily; those of us, loving the country, but living now on the fringe of a city's busyness, must deliberately plan to respond to the Master's invitation, *'Come apart into a quiet place.'*

It requires more than just a quiet place – one must be aware of God in that place, and be in a mood for contemplation. Of one such experience, I wrote:

> The muted orchestra of earth plays on
> as I drowse in these waist-high grasses,
> leaving the busy world to spin
> and the green beetle to go up
> slender grass-stalks.
>
> Colours all around are cool –
> gentlest of greens, browns, pool-blues,
> tall shadows spilling through to
> quietness – sun's bright splinters
> all but shut out.
>
> Healing for tired body is here,
> hidden from the traffic of hate
> and the hot voices of headlines,
> bringing new strength for tomorrow
> when I must go back.
>
> R.F.S.

I am not sure where Mrs Fisher found her 'quiet', when her husband was Archbishop and she was caught up in a busy life; but I remember how she spoke of it over the BBC: 'There have been occasions,' said she, 'when the number and complexity of things to be done seemed overwhelming – days when loyalties seemed to conflict, and I could not decide what to do, or how, nor when to do it. At those times, I found that if I went away somewhere quiet, and knelt down, and literally laid it all out in God's presence, and resigned the puzzle to Him, He did, as it were, give it all back to me in a quiet way. Whenever I find myself looking all tense and screwed-up, I try to get a few minutes' quietness, so as to let go my strain and tension. I am sure that quiet, unfussy people bring peace and restfulness to others in this world which needs peace so badly.'

Three times in the last few years – when I've sought

out 'quiet' for myself countless times – I have led a 'Quiet Day' for a group of church women. The first was a Methodist group; the second a group from the Cathedral; the third, a mixed group. In no one of them, as a cynic might suppose, did we stop talking in one place, and go and talk in another. Any talk there was, was mostly by myself, as leader, since I felt we might be embarrassed by too-long periods of quiet, if not offered some help – not being mystics, or long-time contemplatives. In the first gathering – we met mid-morning in a Baptist camp house, in company with great trees, and a purling stream and much grass – every footstep 'gentled' on that green sward. I shared at intervals thoughts on the Lord's Prayer. The words were well-known, but it was one area of our faith we have become casual about. A fresh approach could be nothing but helpful. I went early to the camp house to prepare our meeting place – a small table drawn up, lots of low chairs and cushions around, with a tiny sprig of flower in a vase, and the slim cross from my study on the table. In the case of the Cathedral group, we met in the mellow wooden Chapel of St Stephen, built by Bishop Selwyn, our country's first bishop. On this occasion, I had no preparations of place to do – only I counted it seemly to wear my preaching-gown. It was a beautiful calm morning – as, indeed, the other had been in the country at the camp house. On the third occasion, we went back to that meeting place, but with a different New Testament passage on which to guide our contemplation.

We gathered, in each case, at mid-morning; and dispersed at mid-afternoon, so that those who had to meet small children from school, and get a meal, could manage. I explained at once, each time, what we meant to do, after we had each given her name, so that, from the start, there would be no loss of ease. No one had been obliged to come – as president, secretary or treasurer of her society; nobody, I explained, was obliged to stay the whole of any one session, if she felt she wanted to quietly rise, and slip out for a walk, or to seek a quiet place alone. (No one did, as each Quiet Day went through. I asked only that anyone moving should respect the quiet of others.)

At midday break, a kettle was boiled by one of our number, and we ate sandwich lunches. No organization was called for, so each was free to share fully in our time together. I broke up each study into six five-minutes of comment each time, and as long a time of quiet; with a lengthy period of quiet at the end, before the Benediction.

With a further cup of tea, before setting off for home, we made time for any comments forthcoming on the worth of the day – centred as it was on utmost simplicity, utmost practicality. One or two spoke briefly – no minutes were kept, of course; no report would be given to any committee to whom we were usually responsible – what there was of worth in the experience, was to be in itself. Others – when they got home – wrote to me. One spoke of it as 'the most wonderful relaxation and refreshing I've ever known'; another wrote : 'I felt that we were part of something bigger than ourselves'. And indeed, we were – an experience of God, though all might not be able to put it into words. A third – a charming young mother of two small children – wrote : 'I had such a scramble to be with you all, away from the children. I was so busy – which now, I know, was the very reason why I needed to be there.' And as a postscript, she penned Moffatt's rendering of Our Lord's words (Matthew 11:28) : 'Come unto Me ... *and I will refresh you!'*

We are a busy people – telephone, radio, TV, and talk; and traffic-noises, with the stutter of pneumatic road-drills occasionally added out of doors, and the weekend concatenation of grass-mowers.

We need from time to time to find 'quiet', to quicken our awareness of God !

22. WHY DO WE SUFFER?

What would happen if suffering knocked in the night?
It may not face us then, of course. W. H. Auden reminds
us of this. In a verse 'About Suffering', he is quite factual;
he says : 'It takes place while someone else is eating or
opening a window or just walking dully along.'

But whenever it comes, suffering is something to be
reckoned with.

I know this. Once – in my eager twenties – for nine
months on end I was confined to my bed, and the doctor
stepped over my doorstep daily. (I had already known
suffering in my 'teens, with a desperate scald – but this
was different.) Kindly neighbours came in, as the news
spread. I soon gave up counting how many times I heard,
in a different voice, the same opening sentence : 'You
p-o-o-r dear! Why should this have happened to you?' I
was too sick to answer. The inference seemed to be that,
since I was doing a useful piece of social work in the
community smitten with an economic crisis, I should
somehow have been immune to the outcome of germs,
chills and accidents. The fact that I was Christian, serving
through the Church, only added to the problem.

The fact was I had been receiving and sorting old
clothes to give away, and I had picked up a germ on the
lining of my heart – 'The kind of germ', I learned, along
with its impressively long name, 'that lodges in dirty
places'. At first, it seemed only a heavy cold. I went home
to bed – it was pleurisy, perhaps? When the doctor came,
his first question was, 'Where have you been?' 'In bed
here, for a week', was my reply. 'But before that?' And
the story of the crowded old-clothes room came out. 'I
want you to stay in bed – still, perfectly still – quite flat –
no moving about – and I'll come tomorrow', were his
parting words.

He came on the morrow; and again on the morrow, and
took my friend aside, and said : 'This is going to be a long

job. How are you placed? Are you here alone?'

'Yes,' answered my friend, quietly, 'but I can nurse her. I have my job here – I'm a teacher of music. I'm also the housekeeper – my mother is away; and I'm Dominion Secretary of the Presbyterian youth movement, that keeps me often late at night – but we'll manage somehow.' Brave words!

I learned slowly the cost of living in my body. Specialists who were consulted wondered if I'd ever work again – one of them said, 'walk again'. But I did.

And in time, I learned a new craft – I wrote a book; but all through increasingly crowded years, I've carried those scars on my heart. Every doctor I have been obliged to consult on my world journeys remarks on this; including the Harley Street specialist, whose doorstep I crossed to please a nurse friend. I found myself fortunate to live in my own country – where much can now be done to help.

Buy a car – and the world seems full of cars; give birth to a baby, or a book, and the world seems full of them; suffer, and the world seems full of sufferers. I still cannot give an answer to the question asked me by so many so freely in those first days – but, I think perhaps I have become a little more compassionate. One thing has become increasingly clear to me – *no glib answers will do!*

I know, of course, as does any wide-awake person, that there is a great deal of suffering in this world. The problem presents itself in all sorts of ways : 'Why should this have happened to me?' 'Why doesn't God do something about it – stop cruel men and women from causing further suffering?' Those who approach the problem thus are plainly by-passing one of the basic conditions of our human free will. God took the risk of giving us this gift – when He might have made us puppets, and settled things Himself. Only the lawless, selfish, and cruel might then have acted – and suffered. But He did not set His world of men and women to work that way.

Volumes have been written on suffering, since the beginning of things, and are still written. I have a few on my shelves, and I've read many more. My own contribution to the pile has been, to date, to add another by way of answer to that primal question. The best I have attempted – and will perhaps ever attempt – has been a slender book of prayers and meditations for the use of the suffering at home, or in hospital, called, *When My Visitors Go*, published by Fontana (Collins) in London. In its Preface I was pleased to be able to write one thing plainly – on the authority of Jesus – *Suffering is not to be reckoned punishment for sin.* He talked freely to those about Him, of the men on whom the Tower of Siloam fell : 'Think ye that they were sinners above all men who dwelt in Jerusalem? I tell you, *"Nay!"* ' (Luke 13 :4-5).

Suffering, like the rain, falls on the just and the unjust – otherwise religion would become an insurance policy. It would pay one in terms of bodily security – and Christianity has never promised that. Our Master Himself came all too soon to suffering, and a cruel death; many of His closest apostles knew persecution, and some, in time, martyrdom, one impaled on a cross, upside down.

Matthew Arnold, nearer our day, felt moved to speak with realism about the good and the true :

> Streams will not curb their pride
> The just man not to entomb
> Nor lightnings go aside
> To give his virtues room;
> Nor is that wind less rough
> Which blows a good man's barge.

Somebody gave me Dr Leslie Weatherhead's *Why Do Men Suffer?* (S.C.M. Press), and it is still on my shelf. He had dedicated it to his loved mother and sister, 'whose bodies were defeated in the battle against painful disease; but who, from defeat, wrested a spiritual victory . . .' The vastness of the problem of suffering baffles still many of us, busy ministers, and social workers, not to mention doctors and nurses. And because it is no respecter of persons we all have to give some deep, sincere thought to it, at some time. We live in our bodies – we belong to the human family – if we miss suffering ourselves, there are any number of others with whom we live, work, worship, and read our day's newspapers, who know it.

I have come now to the place where I believe it is best to recognize that *God built this world on a family basis.* This way, *unearned good* comes to us all – nursing and medical skills at birth, the provision of a home, and soon a school, with picture books and playgrounds, teachers and soon a share in the cumulative knowledge and delight of the culture into which we have been born. We pay no price for this – it is all unearned good. Beginning with nursery rhymes, and tiny, lilting songs, we find our way into the wealth of music which the world holds – in our own country, and every other, of this age and every other. And in this miraculous era of flight, musicians come freely to share what they count priceless, and glorious! All unearned good! This sense of immense beauty comes to me – not only when I hush my heart in Beethoven's little house in Bonn, and look at his collection of instruments, and ear-trumpets, trying to combat his deafness – and then in London, or in my own city hall, or on the wireless, or on records in our own home, revel in the music he gave us. Or I spend a morning in Mozart's house, tucked away no distance from the spire of St Stephen's Church, in Vienna. It surrounds a courtyard, with a pump central at the base of the stairs, which must have been a lively gathering place for gossip. But that little house, where there was never money enough, was the centre of some of the most delightful music in my life – *all unearned good!* And the same must be said of my debt to painters, authors, dramatists, poets – *all unearned good!* This is mine because God built the world on a family basis.

But, conversely, comes also *unearned ill.* Suffering cannot be avoided, if we live where men quarrel, and make war; if men leave foul drains untended, fevers affecting us all will result; if neighbours drown their wits in drink, life will not be the same for any of us; if drivers are reckless in charge of motors, suffering will result. The words of Scripture are unquestioned, 'No man liveth unto himself!'

Added to this is the drugtaking selfishness of many in

our day; the ignorant desire for so-called 'freedom'; the hasty choice on many levels. Acute suffering often comes that way.

And because we live amidst material things, there is always the possibility of plain ignorance, and accidents. A slippery step can bring down one's best friend – and carelessness of other kinds affects others. One can also unwittingly break health laws.

And there are those causes of widespread suffering – tidal waves, landslides, earthquakes, and the like. (Some, in earlier times, we never even heard about, till long after they were dealt with; these days, through the media, we hear of them in all their terror, even while they are happening – and it seems that there are many more, and worse. But it is not necessarily so.) Sometimes, this source of suffering is aggravated by man's desire to live in places that are plainly unfit for habitation. One sunset, aboard ship, Mount Etna came into view, to us as we watched, awe-inspiring, casting off a mantle as we stood silent. On the morrow, we knew, we would walk in fertile Italy and, we hoped, enjoy her fruits and vines.

But before we forsook our darkened deck that velvety night, an unforgettable sight was ours. Our captain drew in towards it, as nearly as he dared, and with all but our mooring lights extinguished. As our eyes became accustomed to the darkness, we managed to pick up the cone-like outline of Stromboli, rising from the sea. Presently, she flung up great burning chunks into the sky; and as we watched, they rolled down sizzling into the sea. With a heavy roll of smoke from the crater, it was a sight, our captain confessed, that brought him real anxiety for the safety of the islanders asleep at that hour – nine o'clock – on the non-eruptive side of the volcano. And it was impossible to look at that home of vine-growers using patches of fertile soil there, without sharing a like concern. When I expressed my fears, our captain said : 'Oh, they say, "It never bursts out on our side of the broken crater." And that, despite the fact that in the past few years, boats from Naples have several times been summoned hurriedly to take them off. Always they come back !'

I cannot think that the lower slopes of temperamental Stromboli are a safe place for people to live. The district of Nelson, where I grew up, was known to be on an earthquake seam – but in the city building laws took this into consideration. (Out in the country, a school-mate of mine was killed when her family home collapsed during the Nelson-Murchison 'Quake.) Suffering, as the result of living in such unsafe places, can't be blamed on God. Reasonable forethought is the responsibility of all of us who build – we must profit by painful experience.

To connect suffering with sin is, to this day, a grievous and mistaken thing to do. There are so many other factors. Faced with 'a man blind from birth', the disciples long ago asked our Master: 'Who did sin, this man, or his parents, that he was born blind?' Jesus answered: *'Neither . . . !'* (John 9 : 1-3). But men and women continue to ask the same painful question. To be religious is not to be immune. Suffering comes to us all at some time or other. 'But surely', say some, 'if God is omnipotent, He could intervene.' And Mill's famous, or rather *infamous*, argument gets another airing: 'Either God is good, and not powerful, or He is powerful, and not good.' But this is too glib an answer, when the God concerned is none other than *the God of Whom Jesus spoke*, in Whom He utterly believed, and to Whom He raised His voice on the Cross, as life ebbed: 'Father, into Thy hands I commit My spirit!'

So old is the problem of suffering! It is a mistake to think that we have only to keep on, and we can find all the answers, like parcels neatly wrapped, and nicely tied. These days we have escaped the full score of suffering men once knew – but suffering of mind, and spirit, are everywhere amongst us still. Up through the years, one saintly soul has said: 'Thou canst not sigh a sigh, and Thy Maker is not nigh.' This is meaningful in our home, however poetical it sounds. My house-friend and I have several times had reason to know it. Standing beside me in illness, she has many more times herself had to enter hospital – twice for cancer operations, not counting foot operations, and once for a new hip. One gets over suffering, of course – but never over the experience of having suffered. Something is added for ever more. This is not to speak lightly. Suffering need not be wasted – some flowers of character flourish that way. But without a deep-down trust in God, Whom Jesus trusted, I cannot see how one can triumph.

23. DO MIRACLES STILL HAPPEN?

There are people, I know, whose question is : 'Did they ever happen?'

They are featured in the Bible, of course – in the Old Testament, but more notably in the New. Some readers have even gone to the point of counting them. 'The four Gospels', says Dr G. R. H. Shafto, in his book *The Wonders of the Kingdom,* 'record some thirty-five incidents in the life of Jesus to which the word "miracle" has been applied.' He is not prepared to sort them out in chronological order – not that that matters – but it is striking that our Master's first act of public ministry should be an occasion for a miracle. He was guest at a wedding. A problem of hospitality arose – and He turned water into wine. As Augustine said : 'We take for granted the slow miracle whereby water in the irrigation of a vineyard becomes wine. It is only when Christ turns water into wine, in quick motion, as it were, that we stand amazed.'

In earlier times, perhaps, it was easier for folk to believe in miracles. Then, they were counted seals upon the record, proofs of God's greatness, Christ's divinity, a support of faith. The difficulty now arises, some feel, out of the fact that science has taught us that the universe is governed by Natural Law. And since God the Creator has designed things that way, it is argued, He cannot break His law.

Defining 'Miracle' as 'something beyond human power to perform, or human mind to understand', many are unready to accept any miracle, although recorded in Scripture. 'It would mean', they argue, 'that God, and His Son, would be guilty of a violation of Natural Law in the world, or at least, "a suspension" of it.'

But to suggest that God *cannot* intervene in this world that He has made, is to reduce Him to a state poorer than our own; for we can, and do, modify the order and speed of events. 'The Christian reply', says Dr G. F. Hunter, 'is that we ourselves change the course of things *by using the laws of Nature*, not by violating them.' And if we can do that, with the little handful of laws we understand, *how much more can God, and Christ!*

Even a child knows that if he takes a handful of paper, cloth, framework of sticks, and string, and throws them up into the air, they will come down on his head, because of the law of gravitation. But if, according to another law of the universe, he fashions those same things – paper, cloth, sticks and string – into a kite, and throws them into the air in that form, they will not fall on his head, but will fly. The shipbuilder knows, as well as anyone, that a lump of steel will sink – it is the law; but he also knows that if he uses another law of the universe, given by the same Creator, and fashions his steel in a certain way, that steel can be counted on to float as a great vessel. In the childhood of many of us there were no aeroplanes above our heads; no wireless sets in our homes, bringing us the words of people we have never seen, some on the other side of the world. Now our TV can do even more – show us their faces, as they speak, though they are as far away. And medical science has presented us with breath-taking miracles, in the same interval of time.

In one of his valued 'News Letters', John Taylor, C.M.S. Secretary, writes of 'the fallacy which finds more of God in the special and the unusual than in the general and the everyday. It is a mistake', he says, 'to think that there is more of God in a healing by laying-on-of-hands than in a healing by surgery.'

Several known to me, having had much pain, each walk now, after an operation, with the aid of an artificial hip, totally without pain. Again and again, a living cornea has been grafted upon a sightless eye, so that the glory of shape and colour has become once more the gift to those who would otherwise walk in darkness. And it has happened that more than one heart has been scraped of harmful accretions whilst still beating, or been massaged again into activity when it has stopped.

One morning, a few years back, Mr Russell Miller of Whitley Bay sat twiddling the knobs of his radio receiving set. Suddenly, he picked up a faint SOS. He managed to grasp that it was being sent from Vienna. That Austrian 'ham', it seemed, was relaying the message from Poland. There, in the city of Warsaw, a little girl of two was seriously ill with inflammation of the lungs. Hospital doctors tending her were doing all they could – but they lacked one drug, *sigmanycin*, nor had they any idea where they could get it in a hurry. The best they could do was to get a message sent out, in the hope that someone somewhere might pick it up. They had never, of course, heard of a place, on the rim of England's map, called Whitley Bay, much less of a Mr Miller, devoted to radio.

Amateur though he was, the moment he picked up the faint message, he hurried to the local police station. And in no time, they managed to get a line through to Scotland Yard. Officers there, in turn, phoned a certain wholesale drug suppliers' office. Others, to save time, made plans for a plane to stand by. So it happened that soon the precious drug was being hurried to the airport by police car, and, with all who could hasten its mission alerted, on its way to do what it could to save a little child's life in far-away Warsaw. *A modern miracle!*

God, Who knows the universe perfectly, must will such miracles, to meet the need of His people as they pray, without violating any law of nature.

And His Son, Jesus – doing His caring Will perfectly and lovingly – could do no less. 'In many of His works of healing', as Hunter adds, 'Our Lord seems to do swiftly and easily what our doctors do painfully and slowly. It is possible that, if they knew as much of the secrets of nature as He did, their cures might be as swift and easy as His. If miracles are possible', concludes Hunter, 'there could be no more fitting occasion for them than in the ministry of the Son of God.'

One thing is impressive, as one looks at His miracles more closely – the fact that *not one of them* was performed for His own comfort, or glory, but for the help of those about Him, and the glory of God His Father. Using a miracle He might have escaped the Cross – He said as much, in the Garden of Gethsemane, when soldiers came to arrest Him, and in that moment of crisis, one of His disciples drew a sword, and struck off an ear of the High Priest's servant. Said Jesus : 'Thinkest thou that I cannot now pray to My Father, and He shall presently give Me more than twelve legions of angels?' (Matthew 26:53). Twelve legions of angels instead of twelve unsteady disciples! One would have been enough. But He did *not* pray for that extra-special help, and He did not get it. Earlier on, when He knew thirst, He might have asked His Father, Creator of all the streams and springs of earth, for water to drink – but He didn't. He sat at midday, on a wellside, and asked a woman there to give Him a drink. Fatigued, on another occasion, at the long, crowded day's end, He might have asked for miracle refreshment of body and mind – but He didn't; He slept on a cushion in the end of Peter's fishing-boat. He never resorted to miracles for Himself – but He used them widely for the relief of men and women about Him.

And there is in each one of them recorded, something very different from the grotesque 'wonder-workings' which occur in the Apocryphal Gospels – like stories of giving flight and song to clay birds. These all lack the usefulness, dignity and relevancy of Jesus's miracles.

And looking ahead – as He did whilst He took His last supper with His disciples in the Upper Room – He said to them : 'Believe Me that I am in the Father, and the Father in Me; or else believe Me for the very work's sake. Verily, verily, I say unto you, he that believeth on Me, the works that I do shall he do also; *and greater works than these shall he do; because I go unto My Father.*' (John 14:11-12). Remarkable words!

Dr John A. T. Robinson, Bishop of Woolwich and author of *Honest to God*, says in another book of his, in our day : 'The miracles are seen by Jesus, not as things He alone could do because He was divine, but as what any man could do who was really open to the love and power of God.'

In these days, we are gradually moving from the totally physical approach to illness, even where the illness seems to us physical. Can it be that we are on the verge of acknowledging something that Jesus fully knew? Our term *psychosomatic* – on the lips of all our doctors, nurses, and lay helpers – is derived from two Greek words meaning 'mind' and 'body', and we work now from the premise that both belong together – a sick person is one whole. From doctors with whom I've had dealings, I have heard instances of what seem like miraculous recovery, when a patient has been helped beyond emotional upset, to deal with guilt, and to know deep down the wonder of forgiveness.

And there are amongst us miracles of other kinds – God never meant us to go far without stumbling on a miracle! We must keep our critical faculties alive – but no less, our sense of awe. There is no denying that in this universe of God's, miracles happen – as they happened in the ministry of Jesus – and not only in those experiences bearing the accepted term 'miracle'. One of the greatest was surely His transformation of Peter – a roughly-spoken, impulsive fisherman – into Peter the apostle; and the bringing together in love, and service, of that bunch of men, so strikingly different that they argued among themselves *who should be greatest*, even as they came up to Jerusalem, and into the Upper Room, with the Master facing crucifixion. Miracles of personality are, perhaps, the greatest of all miracles. Among my friends is an artist – greying now in the service of Christ – who was a few years ago, an alcoholic. Today, he is 'a walking miracle'.

Part of our modern *malaise* is that we have grown casual about many things. We need to open our eyes to see. Says one among us:

> If the good God were suddenly
> To make a solitary Blind to see
> We would stand wondering all
> And call it *miracle*:
> But that He gives with lavish hand
> Sight to a million souls, we stand
> And say, with little awe,
> He but fulfils a natural law!

24. IS CONSCIENCE THE VOICE OF GOD?

'It was the Stoics who invented for us the term "conscience"', said Dr C. H. Dodd, 'and it is their permanent contribution to ethics.' For all that, we must not credit it with being more than it is – the Voice of God. It is not. Rather is it 'a tutor', to help us on our rightful way. Situations in which we find ourselves having to act with decision are always a mixture of right and wrong. It is rarely possible to see our way, and know what to do unaided.

Young Huckleberry Finn could only say: 'Conscience takes up more room than all the rest of a person's insides.' A quaint way of putting the matter! Another I find, asserting as confidently: 'A good conscience often makes one feel bad'. And moving out of youth into adulthood, Charles Morgan, in our day, introduces us to one of his characters, and what we hear him saying, is: 'Conscience is a pretty swerving beast in me, anyway.'

However we define conscience, there are times when it is immature, and ill-informed. That was Saul's trouble, before his dramatic experience on the Damascus Road. To the best of his ability, he believed his actions were right, and serving God, when he set off zealously to persecute the early Christians. It was only after his change of allegiance and name – from Saul to Paul – that he came to realize how perverted his conscience was. And it was a continuing grief to him.

But one thing is plain: a lively conscience never errs on two points – always it sees that there is a difference between right and wrong; and always it admits that one must *do* the right, whatever its cost.

There are situations, as Paul learned, that can be very costly. Paul's acceptance of all that his new allegiance involved brought him up against former enemies – some of whom still retained their suspicion of him. Others made it necessary for him to escape through a window in a high

wall, let down in a basket. Others again brought him
before the court, and got him thrown into prison. He
came to suffer lashes, loneliness, shipwreck. But however
costly, the result of his meeting with Christ was never
questioned – he knew he could not turn back.

On one occasion, required to speak his mind, he found
words to say : 'Herein do I exercise myself, to have always
a conscience void of offence toward God, and toward men.'
(Acts 24 : 16). And there is no missing the order of pro-
cedure : first God, then men.

Many people since have suffered because of conscience.
As Dr Harry Fosdick reminds us : 'Galileo, standing for
the truth under persecution, was conscientious, but so,
too, were his persecutors . . . They had no selfish ends to
serve in persecuting Galileo – they did it for conscience'
sake.' Lecky, in his *History of European Morals*, says :
'Philip II and Isabella . . . inflicted more suffering in
obedience to their consciences than Nero and Domitian in
obedience to their lusts.'

So it is a risk, and a responsibility, to be possessed of
this gift, conscience. It is so easily drugged with self-
justification. It is the area where young Christians feel
earliest that they must operate, for good or ill. 'The test
of a Church', Dr Hensley Henson liked to say, 'is *the kind
of conscience* it creates in its members.' My phone rang
lately, and when I lifted the receiver, it was to hear the
manager of my favourite bookshop. Said he : 'If you've
a minute to spare, I think you'll be interested in this . . .'
I encouraged him to go on. 'I was busy here last evening,
when a young fellow came in. "Two years ago," said he,
"I stole two books from your shop." Taken aback, I asked :
"Do you remember the titles?" "Yes," came his prompt
answer, "and I remember the prices they were marked.
I've become a Christian in the meanwhile, *and I've come
to pay you for them.*"

'With that explanation,' said my friend, 'he handed
over a banknote. "But that's much too much," I replied.
"No", said he, "I have to pay fourfold." '

Over the phone, we talked of his decision. Restitution,
of course, is a good thing – but why fourfold? 'Perhaps,'

I argued, 'the young Christian had been hearing a sermon on Nathan's words of long ago that had made David squirm? "He shall restore the lamb *fourfold*, because he did this thing!' (2 Samuel 12 :6). Or perhaps he had been confronted with the New Testament story of Zacchaeus. Called down out of a wayside tree under which Jesus passed, in Jericho, to receive Him as guest, Zacchaeus had been led to make a little speech, as He crossed his threshold : "If I have taken anything from any man . . . I will restore him *fourfold*." ' (Luke 19 :8).

I had no way of being sure – for no one knows how God works in a human soul. My friend's book-till is now a handsome sum richer; with a young Christian's pay-envelope the same amount poorer.

Like all other faculties, conscience needs to be disciplined and sensitized. And it takes time. I've been hearing of a young fellow countryman – an officer who served in Bensberg, West Germany, after the war. When it was time to leave, he thought he'd like to take home with him a souvenir. So he got the use of a tall ladder and climbing up a memorial there, plucked a bronze leaf from a wreath held by the Goddess of Peace. At that moment, he felt very pleased with his effort.

But years on, a successful businessman in my country, he began to feel less pleased with his spirited prank, and in time, even less so. It lay on his conscience. For a long time he could do nothing about it. Then it became possible to plan a trip to Europe. Now, outstanding among his memories of that trip, is his return to Bensberg – and the chance it gave him to restore the bronze leaf he had lifted years before. Happily – though they were not aware that it was missing – the townsfolk entered into the spirit of the matter on their visitor's conscience. They invited him, along with his wife and family, to be guests of their town.

One can't report that all actions of the kind, prompted by conscience, turn out so well – one would wish they might – but in any case, it is the *new peace* that comes to the offender that matters. Once more, he feels right.

To match this kind of need – widespread – Courts of

Conscience first made their appearance at Westminster; later, in other places, supported by local acts of parliament. Usually these were for the recovery of small sums, almost always under five pounds. And the common term, *Conscience money* came into usage, to cover the sums received from people who wished to remain anonymous in clearing their consciences. This remains a useful term, the Taxation Department assures us. Every year, it seems, somebody has trouble with his taxes. Sir Heneage Ogilvie of Guy's Hospital has underlined this, in a delightful story.

'I had repaired a hernia in an old farmer,' said he, 'and presented him with a bill for thirty pounds. That was ordinary enough. But, on receipt of it, the old fellow opened a locker, and pulled out a cigar-box and started to count out some dirty pound notes.

' "Look here", I said, "you will want your ready cash for wages; why not give me a cheque?"

' "Oh, no, sir", replied the old patient, *"this'll suit me better for income tax. I'll put you down as a load of manure!"* '

Conscience sets up a battle with subterfuge – being what the Oxford Dictionary defines as 'the moral sense of right and wrong'. And who need add more, on this important matter, save to repeat, *it is not the voice of God*. Though it is awareness of God that gives us our standard of values, our basis for behaviour.

25. HOW MUCH CAN A SHRUG ACCOMPLISH?

One learns a language early in life; but with the years, it
is discovered to be subject to change. New words are
added and others, long-established, drop out. Some of
them we can ill afford to lose. 'Compassion' is one such;
my dictionary defines it as 'pity, inclining one to spare or
help'. Not surprisingly, it appears again and again in the
Gospels. One reads in the first of them ever assembled
(Mark 1 :41), 'Jesus, moved with compassion, put forth
His hand . . .' And it is like that all the way – a personal
response, leading to some practical outcome.

This verse walked up and down in my mind, as typical
of His whole ministry, when I knelt a while ago, before
Thorvaldsen's figure of Him in the Protestant Cathedral
in Copenhagen. It was a Communion Service, so I had
the opportunity to kneel before Him, beyond my pew;
and I was glad of that, because somebody, describing the
gracious figure, had said : 'You cannot see His face unless
you kneel at His feet !'

And I saw His hands, too. There is a story of how they
came to be as they are – fitting so well those words of
Mark. It is said that, when the sculptor set about his task,
he made the hands raised high, in majesty. He worked at
the figure for weeks; and when he surveyed it, finished,
felt some satisfaction. So that the clay might set, he closed
the door of his studio for several days. There was a storm.
And when Thorvaldsen returned, it was to find that damp-
ness had invaded the space where it stood, and altered
the statue. His hands, formerly raised in triumph, had
been lowered. The sculptor's first concern was to raise
them again; then, as he looked upon them, bathed in
light, he saw them, instead, reaching out in compassion.

And so they remain – speaking with unforgettable comfort and strength, that reality which Mark set in his simple
words : *'Jesus, moved with compassion, put forth His
hand.'*

How much can a shrug accomplish?

Somebody has called this time in which we live, 'the age of the shrug'. Certainly, there are many amongst us, tired of the constant printed appeals in the newspaper, and through the post, and spoken by wireless, and shown on television. One, summing up the situation, has said:

> We've seen too much
> too long,
> and too often,
> on television,
> and in the morning paper.
> We glance away
> and read
> the engagements.
>
> Too many bodies in the jungle,
> too many protests at home,
> refugees everywhere,
> epidemics and floods,
> typhoons and disasters,
> leprosy,
> rags, and tin mugs.
>
> Too many appeals like this one,
> kids suffering,
> pot-bellies,
> match-stick legs,
> eyes large and haunting;
> 'too bad', we say,
> and turn the page . . .

Of course, the task seems colossal, and our resources small. I remember feeling this when I visited Calcutta, and its crowded, beggarly streets. A friend drove me one night to Sealdah Railway station. I'd never been close to anything like it. Men, women, and little children were huddled there, as the only place where they could breathe, and be, after the partition of India and Pakistan. Those I looked down upon were making pathetic 'homes' on the pavement of the station, between bricks placed end-to-end, to make each family a space, like children do, playing houses. In full sight of all who passed, or stood appalled, as I did, all the cooking, and crying, and the sweet sanctities of family life went on. This, I learned, was the only little bit of space earth could afford them; and some had already been there *years*!

Shortly afterwards, a hundred families were moved by the Christian churches of the world, to a refugee settlement they had established. At first, they had to manage with tents; then bricks were given them, along with other simple building materials, with someone to offer them expert supervision. One Inter-Church Aid helper told how, laughing and weeping, as were most of them, one of their old ladies bent down, and kissed the feet of the young minister sent by the Church, to be their deliverer.

On the Sunday evening, I led the worship in a fine Mission church, centring my utterance, when I had to preach, on the first two words of the prayer we shared, 'Our Father . . .' And when it came time to go to another appointment, I stepped, to my horror, over the prostrate sleeping body of 'my brother', in the street-gutter. That great sweltering city, in the night – once known as 'The City of Palaces' because of its pretentious public buildings, and grand private homes – had become cursed with appalling slums, and an estimated million pavement dwellers.

I did not then know of Mother Teresa, and her Christ-like compassion; and I had to wait till she came to my own country, to quicken our sense of obligation. It was my privilege to spend some time alone with her, and to hear a little more than I had read by this time, of the compassion shown by the founder of *The Missionaries of Charity* and her devoted Catholic helpers, to the bewildered and dying in Calcutta. She was not, I discovered, an Indian herself, but had been born of Albanian parents in Yugoslavia. Part of her religious training had been taken in Ireland; sent then, to her soul's joy, to begin her novitiate in Darjeeling. In 1948, she had requested permission to live outside the cloister, and work in the Calcutta slums. Rome agreed; and laying aside her

Loreto habit for a cheap sari with a blue stripe as border, that has ever since been the uniform of compassion to many, she became an Indian citizen.

Since then she has, in truth, become a world citizen, travelling in many parts – in India, after initial difficulties, with the help of the interested Minister of Railways personally. In time, she earned as well the support, in her work, of Calcutta's experienced Police Commissioner. By this, countless lay people, and leaders of all sections of the world Church – and some with no connection – came to her aid. Now, her compassionate work was spread over many countries – reaching, as no one till that moment had been able to do so tellingly, 'the poorest of the poor'.

I learned that Mother Teresa had become responsible for eighty-one schools in India alone; thirty-five mobile dispensaries; twenty-eight family planning centres; and in all, sixty-seven leprosy clinics; twenty-eight homes for abandoned children; thirty-two homes for the dying. All this, and more, adds up to be impressive – to be what Mother Teresa calls in her own simple way, 'A vocabulary of Love'. She is fond of saying how the poor – needing more than food and shelter – must be made to know deep-down that 'they are human beings, and wanted'. She is fond of saying that 'welfare is for a purpose – a necessary one – whereas love is for a person'.

How humbly she moves about in her cotton sari! How warm is her heart! How tender, and practical, her hands! Nobody has yet attempted to write her full biography – Malcolm Muggeridge managed a part, that he called *Something Beautiful for God*, from one of her favourite sayings. The day-to-day, year-to-year unceasing service made possible by many working together, in many places, is her story. And meanwhile, she doesn't desire any other. Her whole life is 'Pity, inclining one to spare or help', 'Compassion, in Christ's name'.

26. WHAT SHALL WE THINK OF DEATH?

Or shall we try *not* to think of it? Dr Coggan, Archbishop of Canterbury, addressing the Royal Society of Medicine, lately spoke of this conspiracy of silence concerning death. He wants dying, he says, 'to be as good an act as preparation, skill and love can make it'.

This, I feel, is just to be sensible – not morbid or gloomy – since this is a fact we are not invited to argue about. Once it was the thing to speak much of death – too much – and nothing of sex. Now, the order has changed – much is written and spoken of sex, and little or nothing of death. Dr Paul Tillich reports, as he looks around : 'Our basic anxiety is the fear of death.' It is true, many do their best even to avoid the term. They speak instead of 'losing somebody', of a loved one 'passing away'; others, of a poetical turn of mind, speak of 'the dreaded extinguisher of Life's little candle'.

From time to time my phone brings me news of the death of someone I know; the post carries a letter to my box; or the daily newspaper draws my attention to a name, set in the centre of a few words of print. Some of these are Christian, some not. 'The Gospel', as Dr Herbert Farmer says, 'is indeed a message concerning a great revelation, a great light, but it is *a light which shines out of darkness, not one that banishes it.*' Sometimes my immediate response is to hasten to the home where death has come; or failing that, to join others in a Christian service of memorial. Usually it is in a church, but not always – sometimes it is in a home. A while back, as I voyaged up to Tonga on the *Matua*, I stood one morning with a silent company on deck, ploughing through the Pacific. This was a new experience – yet an ancient one – for it dealt with death. Our vessel seemed so small in that moment : the ocean we sailed exceeding in size all the dry land in the world, every drop of three Atlantics, or, if our choice fell in another direction, seventy Mediterraneans.

And we seemed, as persons, suddenly insignificant. For there, in our silent presence, our captain committed to the depths of that mighty ocean the ashes of the ship's first captain. (None of us passengers, at the time of leaving port, knew that this sacred duty was to be undertaken. Now, here we were mid-morning, facing the reality of death.) The captain read from Paul's letter to the Corinthian Christians, about the essential faith that changes its dark mystery to a reality shot through with divine hope.

And a few weeks ago – at a sunny morning service in a crematorium chapel – the same passage was read within my hearing. The unusual thing, this time, was that the service was held to mark the death of an old lady loved and honoured, in *her hundred-and-third year*! For a long time she had lived with her daughter and son-in-law, with children, and grandchildren growing up around. A little while back, the old lady moved into a nearby church village, with its own hospital. Always attractive, the last birthday on which I visited her she sat up in bed, wearing on the front of her well-tended hair, a tiny pink bow. She was a happy person. Each day the nurses got her up; and each day took her a little walk down the long corridor. Each time she came back, she thanked them, and each time said: 'It's a funny thing, that whenever I go up "the street" these days, I never meet a soul I know.' Wistful! But the truth is, of course, that if one stays here so long, there are few, if any, to meet.

Death has several times come close to me, through the years – with the death, in the Battle of Britain, of my closest friend, Buttons; the sudden death of my mother; of my father; my brother; my brother-in-law; and several others tied to me by the ties of blood, friendship, or obligation.

The New Testament – moving on from the Old, for a moment's thought – has a good deal to say about death. Being the honest book it is, it is bound to have. Not even Our Lord's close friend Lazarus, in the home He visited most often, was exempt. He was young, and full of life's interests – but he died, and, before his friend could arrive, was buried. The Gospel records the story of his grieving sisters, Mary and Martha, amid village folk gathered around. *'Jesus wept!'* (John 11:35). And there is added the ageless word of consolation to the sisters in their grief, spoken by Jesus – and it reaches us now in our need. Said He : *'I am the Resurrection and the Life!'*

This was new to the ears of men and women. And now, those of us who must tearfully face the experience of death have no need to manage without it. It isn't, of course, much to say; but coming from Him, it is enough. *'Because I live'*, said He later, *'you too shall live!'* (John 14:19).

On the question of whether or not a person who is soon to die should be told, or surrounded with kindly optimism, flinging off references to gardening, cooking, picnicking next week, there is a difference of opinion. Some, to spare themselves if not their patient, like to pretend. Even whilst this approach is being held, the patient may well be aware of the deception. The result is lack of support – which is possible only when there is a relationship based on truth. Many a patient, I know, would welcome deep-down talk on this basic experience, often so studiously avoided by doctor, relatives and friends. Some among the sick, it is argued, would immediately give up any 'fight' they might be expected to put up, if they knew they were irrevocably moving toward death. They say it is a matter of temperament. Perhaps so? Since death, as I see it from a Christian point of view, is not *extinction*, but the way *to a larger experience*, I know I would sooner be treated faithfully. 'No matter', says a writer in a medical journal I occasionally see, 'how humane the approach of many of us is, is it proper *to deprive a person of his death*?' This is only in the *conscious sense* of its on-coming, of course. There is no other choice open to us. And in our human experience, as time ticks by, it seems to carry a terrible sense of finality. Ernest Rhys shows that as plainly as can be, in 'Jo's Requiem' :

> He had the ploughman's strength
> in the grasp of his hand :
> He could see a crow
> three miles away,

and the trout beneath the stone.
He could hear the green oats growing,
and the south-west wind making rain.
He could hear the wheel upon the hill
when it left the level road.
He could make a gate, and dig a pit,
and plough as straight as stone can fall.
And he is dead.

But the Christian will not accept that as the last word, real as it is. There is no by-passing death.

Medical science these days has miraculously lengthened out our days – but death must be reckoned with, nevertheless. Still faith is a factor. Many a time, visiting one in grave illness, or in advanced age, I have felt like using the words of the old Virginians : 'Come down Death, right easy!' For always I have been praying, under my breath.

After all, *this adventure into the unknown, is into God's known*. When we came into this life, we knew nothing of it; but love had already prepared all that was necessary. For this is God's world – and faith tells us that the next – beyond death – is His, too. His love will not fail. What that larger life will be like, I have no idea – only that it will be centred in the loving being of God. 'There is nothing in the world of which I feel so certain', men and women of his relatively short lifetime were enheartened to hear Dr William Temple say. 'I have no idea what it will be like, and I am glad that I have not. I do not want it . . . as mere continuance, but I want it for my understanding of this life.'

Call death what we will – though surely it is best to call it *death* – it is a tremendous experience. The man or woman who dismisses death lightly has nothing to say to me. Nor has anyone, meeting death, without the sunlit, life-giving words of Jesus. He raised His eyes to look beyond it. And this we too can do, once the glory of His words reaches our inmost hearts. So much rests on His Resurrection !

'Now are we the sons of God', said John in his turn, following faithfully, hopefully, *'and it doth not yet appear*

what we shall be!' (I John 3:2). Expectation grows out
of the Resurrection of Jesus – in God's eternal purpose, it
is all of one glorious piece! 'What we have to grasp is
that the Resurrection is not a lovely afterthought, an ex-
planatory addendum, a mere epilogue, tagged on to the
main story about Jesus', says Dr Murdo Ewen Macdonald,
youngish Scottish preacher of our day. 'It stands', he is
convinced, 'at the centre of the faith, as the axis round
which Christianity revolves. The God Christians believe in
is essentially the Resurrection God. When Peter says,
"Blessed be God the Father of our Lord Jesus Christ Who
hath begotten us again unto a lively hope by the Resurrection of Jesus Christ from the dead", he is speaking for
his fellow apostles, and for the whole of the New Testament.' And he is speaking for millions today – *and for my
own heart.*

27. BELONGING HERE AND NOW

It comes as a surprise that Jesus – as far as our Christian records show – never used the word 'religion'. For all that, it is basic to our approach to life. It may have been that in His day, religion had gathered about it so much that was unreal, unworthy. He chose rather to talk of God the Father, and of *our belonging to Him – sharing His Will in the world.* And there is, to this day, nothing more real.

Dr Herbert Farmer, for all his ease with theological phraseology, turned to simple words to make this glorious reality as plain as possible. 'It is not', says he, 'that God creates a man, and then pops him into a world of persons, as a housewife makes a dumpling and pops it into the saucepan – both dumpling and saucepan being capable of existing apart from one another. To come into existence as a person', he sums up, 'is to be incorporated in this world of the personal, *to be in relation to persons – the Divine Person and human persons – and existence is not possible on any other terms.*' This is, I think, the best definition of 'religion' that I know.

It has to do with all things far and near, with ultimates and intimates. In a psalm familiar to Jesus, and now in the praise psalms at the end of our collection (147:3-4), is one of the loveliest word-portraits of the God to Whom we belong, and to Whom we sing praises. '*He healeth the broken in heart . . . He telleth the number of the stars.*' A breath-taking, supporting reality this!

I never cease to marvel at God's expression of power when, at night, I raise my eyes, to consider His canopy overhead, the psalmist's words in my mind. He challenges me to embrace the two great thoughts at once – for it is only the God Who can count the stars, Who can heal the broken in heart. *He could not meet my intimate need, if the immensity of the stars was beyond Him. But even in these desperately exacting days, I find, He is wholly adequate.* So praise goes on!

John Wesley laid hold of the same dual reality, in his day, and nothing in our jet age has happened to alter this. Said he, 'I see now, that if God's love can reach up to every star, and down to every poor soul on earth, it must be vastly simple; so simple that all dwellers on earth may be assured of it without considering their deserts.' This is a revelation that prompted me to begin this book, and to carry it through to this point, to cover the whole of life.

Some of us have been, at times, liable to belittle the greatness of God. A title chosen for a book on this fact, by Dr J. B. Phillips, startled many. He spoke too straightforwardly. He said, *Your God is Too Small*. Two passages in his Introduction could not be passed by. 'The trouble with many people today', said he, 'is that they have not found a God big enough for modern needs. While their experience of life has grown in a score of directions, and their mental horizons have been expanded to the point of bewilderment by world events and by scientific discoveries, their ideas of God have remained largely static. It is obviously impossible for an adult to worship the conception of God that exists in the mind of a child . . . If, by a great effort of will, he does do this he will always be secretly afraid lest some new truth may expose the juvenility of his faith. And it will always be by such an effort that he either worships or serves a God Who is really too small to command his adult loyalty and co-operation . . .

'*Many men and women today are living, often with inner dissatisfaction, without any faith in God at all. This is not because they are particularly wicked or selfish . . . but because they have not found with their adult minds a God big enough to "account for" life, big enough to "fit in with" the new scientific age.*'

Canon Peter Green of Manchester put it as simply and as straightly, knowing well our modern needs: 'There is no emotion so necessary to a true religion, nor any so fundamental to it, as *the sense of belonging to God.*'

The simple truth is that at all levels of life – made as we are, body, mind and spirit, whether we recognize it or not – light dies out of our eyes, and joyous, on-going purpose out of our days, when we have no sense of belonging. The loosening of family life these days, the secret, daily support of home, first underlines this lack for many. A small child made headline news a while ago in Australian papers. We learned how she had run away from Seaforth Home, Somerton, twice. A deserted child of a broken home, she said simply, that she was 'searching *for someone to belong to*'. At seven years of age, she didn't sit down and think up these words – they were part of her very nature. In family, community, and national sense, they are lastingly true; but at no level more truly than in the realm of the spirit. This isn't something which the Church has thought up; it is a reality that is deeply embedded in our human nature. We are fashioned, as men and women, no less for *togetherness*, than for *separateness*. And life becomes flat, thin, brittle without this belonging – it reaches the deepest places of our nature.

What love does in transfiguring life,
religion does in transfiguring love.
                              Coventry Patmore

ACKNOWLEDGEMENTS

The author is grateful for permission to quote from the following works :

'Nothing is more beautiful . . .' Poem by R. H. Grenville.

'Who is God?' Poem by Raymond Hearn, from *Modern Psalms for Boys*, Hodder & Stoughton Educational Books.

'You must picture me . . .' *Surprised by Joy*, by C. S. Lewis, Geoffrey Bles, 1955; and Fount Paperbacks, 1977, p. 182.

'Think of sunsets . . .' *How to Believe*, by Dr Ralph Sockman, Epworth Press (out of print).

'Whatever else . . .' *God's Way with Men*, by Professor Norman Pittenger, Hodder & Stoughton, 1969, p. 27.

'It would be . . .', 'The Christian Faith . . .' and 'The trouble with many people . . .' *Your God is Too Small*, by J. B. Phillips, Epworth Press, and Macmillan Publishing Co. Inc., 1952.

'In our modern English idiom . . .' by Dr William Barclay.

'How easily my neighbour . . .' Poem by Richard Watson Gilder, 'Credo', source unknown.

'If I were standing . . .' by Lilian McDonald, in *It's My Belief*, affirmations broadcast by the BBC, Epworth Press, 1953, p. 32.

'One of the most solemn facts . . .' by Professor Herbert Butterfield, source unknown.

'When we first set out . . .' by Professor Arnold Toynbee, in the sixth volume of *Study of History*, Oxford University Press, 1939.

'Always there are unmistakable signs . . .' by Dr J. S. Stewart, in *The Wind of the Spirit*, Hodder & Stoughton, 1968, p. 15.

'Who has not carolled Mary?' Poem by Gilbert Thomas, *Collected Poems*, Allen & Unwin, 1969.

'Last night, going to bed . . .' from *An Autobiography* by Edwin Muir, Hogarth Press, 1968.

Acknowledgements

'I stood beside the bed . . .' Poem by Joan Hutson, *The Officer*, The Salvation Army, London and New Zealand.

'When I first went to work . . .' by the Rev. Peter Beere.

'He had the ploughman's strength . . .' 'Jo's Requiem', poem by Ernest Rhys, from *Wales England Wed*, J. M. Dent & Sons (out of print).

Rhys, from *Wales England Wed*, J. M. Dent & Sons (out of print).

Every effort has been made to acknowledge copyright material. Where efforts have failed, apologies are made, with the promise to right matters in any subsequent edition.